"Everyone has an idea of how they'd like their life to look. And everyone, at some point, comes to realize that life doesn't always resemble their intended design. If you find yourself at this juncture—observing the contrast between what is and what was imagined—then *A Redesigned Life* is for you. Just as design books help us decorate our homes, *A Redesigned Life* will acquaint you with God as the Designer of your life and guide you in adorning the home of your heart. Tracy's wisdom and practical tips in these pages will help you uncover balance, space, and contrast in your life and home."

Trina McNeilly, author of *La La Lovely: The Art of Finding Beauty in the Everyday*

"Life is art. Life is beauty. Life is by design—or rather redesign—by a God who meets us in the midst of our disappointments, chaos, and heartaches. In a world where little seems to make sense, Tracy Steel draws our hearts back to a creative Creator who has his sleeves rolled up and is busy making our lives beautiful, even if we can't immediately see it. Tracy's use of design principles opened my eyes to the wonder of God-at-work in a thoughtful and fresh way. This book is a treasure and a gift and one that needs to be shared with a friend or small group!"

Tricia Goyer, *USA Today* bestselling author of more than seventy books, including *Walk It Out: The Radical Result of Living God's Word One Step at a Time*

"We're told, 'Make your plan; then work your plan.' But what happens when your plan doesn't work? In *A Redesigned Life*, Tracy Steel shows us it isn't that our lives aren't working. Our master Designer is simply working out his best plan in and for us, and this is what we can build true confidence on—a confidence that won't fail us when we need it most."

Lynn Cowell, author of *Make Your Move* and speaking and writing team member of Proverbs 31 Ministries

"I was laughing and crying before the end of the first chapter. Encouragement and conviction dripped off the page as I leaned in to hear my friend Tracy's heart. This is a must-read book if you've ever felt like life did not go as planned. Tracy tenderly reminds us that God has designed a better life for us!"

Micah Maddox, author of *Anchored In: Experience a Power-Full Life in a Problem-Filled World*

"With practical suggestions for spiritual growth alongside fun design tips, *A Redesigned Life* will enhance your ability to create beauty in your home and help you identify the beauty of God in your life. Through personal stories and biblical truth, Tracy will enable you to see more clearly who God is and how he can redesign your life."

Katie Orr, author and Bible teacher

"Tracy is the fun-loving, truth-telling BFF we all need, the one who knocks on the door, coffee and paintbrush in hand, to help redecorate your home . . . and while she's there, just might pull out the Bible and help rearrange your heart too. Tracy's Scripture-rich book will keep you snort laughing even as you are soul searching. Whether it's time to spruce up a few rooms in your heart or for a total renovation, this book will help you embrace and enjoy the unique life the great Designer has drawn up for you."

Elizabeth Laing Thompson, author of *When God Says, "Wait"* and *When God Says, "Go"*

"This book is a gentle reminder that the lives our very creative God designs for us are far more beautiful than the ones we try to design for ourselves. Just as rooms in our homes come together through the layering of different elements, so do our lives. Tracy took me on an interior design journey of the heart, and I came out on the other side more aware of the power of my heavenly Father's brushstrokes to paint new life into every corner."

Vanessa Hunt, author of *Life in Season*

"An interior designer turned Bible teacher, Tracy is someone who has discovered purpose in living a life she never planned. In *A Redesigned Life*, she invites us to embrace the ways God moves in our lives in order to discover our true purpose—not to live for ourselves but for the One who died to save us."

Lauren Gaskill, author, speaker, and founder of She Found Joy

"Our hearts are a lot like our homes—so many spaces filled with a myriad of life experiences and, in my case, a few cluttered corners. Just as our homes need to be refreshed or renovated, our hearts and minds need God's transformative touch as well. I love how Tracy identifies all the ways that God masterfully redesigns our lives to bring out our beauty and character, no matter how worried or worn out we may be. Her practical exercises and powerful insights will equip you to discover God's redesigned life for you."

Barb Roose, speaker and author of *Winning the Worry Battle* and *Joshua: Winning the Worry Battle*

"*A Redesigned Life* is a must-read for the woman yearning for beauty within a life that has been upturned by the unexpected. Written through the unique and intriguing lens of design theory, Tracy's book gives us a new way to think about God, one that reflects both his creative nature and his deep affection for humanity. Tracy's infectious love for people and Jesus shines throughout as she weaves solid biblical teaching, engaging personal stories, and practical application tools into twelve chapters that will encourage you to recognize God's work in your life and call it beautiful."

Heather M. Dixon, speaker and author of *Determined: Living Like Jesus in Every Moment*

"Tracy Steel masterfully weaves real life stories with the truth of God's Word. Pulling salient points that match design principles, she encourages Christ followers to run the race well. It's such a joy to have her voice in the marketplace, and I pray that many readers will enjoy and apply the truths found within the pages of *A Redesigned Life: Uncovering God's Purpose When Life Doesn't Go as Planned*."

Victoria Duerstock, musician, speaker, and author of
*Heart & Home: Design Basics for Your Soul and Living
Space* and *Heart & Home for Christmas: Celebrating Joy
in Your Living Space* (September 2019)

"It has been awhile since I've gotten really excited about a book other than the Bible, but *A Redesigned Life* was one I did not want to put down! I loved Tracy's clever comparison of basic interior design principles with the masterful and meaningful design God uses in our lives every day. This book encouraged me—right where I am—to get my eyes off my circumstances and onto the One who works very purposefully in and through me and has designed good plans for me!"

Amy Hale, speaker, influencer, and Bible teacher

"Reading *A Redesigned Life* is like sitting on a comfy couch with a new best friend, sipping hot tea and having a soul-stirring chat. Full of humor, solid biblical examples, personal anecdotes, and practical design tips, *A Redesigned Life* will leave you inspired and equipped to embrace the life God has designed for you—a life full of hope, joy, and a splash of color!"

Jennifer Bleakley, author of *Joey: How a Blind
Rescue Horse Helped Others Learn to See*

A
Redesigned
Life

A Redesigned Life

**UNCOVERING GOD'S
PURPOSE WHEN LIFE
DOESN'T GO AS PLANNED**

Tracy Steel

Revell

a division of Baker Publishing Group
Grand Rapids, Michigan

© 2019 by Tracy Steel

Published by Revell
a division of Baker Publishing Group
PO Box 6287, Grand Rapids, MI 49516-6287
www.revellbooks.com

Printed in the United States of America

Library of Congress Cataloging-in-Publication Data is on file at the Library of Congress, Washington, DC.

978-0-8007-3553-1

Unless otherwise indicated, Scripture quotations are from the Holy Bible, New International Version®. NIV®. Copyright © 1973, 1978, 1984, 2011 by Biblica, Inc.™ Used by permission of Zondervan. All rights reserved worldwide. www.zondervan.com. The "NIV" and "New International Version" are trademarks registered in the United States Patent and Trademark Office by Biblica, Inc.™

Scripture quotations labeled ESV are from The Holy Bible, English Standard Version® (ESV®), copyright © 2001 by Crossway, a publishing ministry of Good News Publishers. Used by permission. All rights reserved. ESV Text Edition: 2016

Scripture quotations labeled GNT are from the Good News Translation in Today's English Version-Second Edition. Copyright © 1992 by American Bible Society. Used by permission.

Scripture quotations labeled NLT are from the Holy Bible, New Living Translation, copyright © 1996, 2004, 2007, 2013, 2015 by Tyndale House Foundation. Used by permission of Tyndale House Publishers, Inc., Carol Stream, Illinois 60188. All rights reserved.

Published in association with Jessica Kirkland and the literary agency of Kirkland Media Management, LLC., P.O. Box 1539, Liberty, Texas 77575

Interior design by Brian Brunsting

19 20 21 22 23 24 25   7 6 5 4 3 2 1

In memory of Foxy Roxie

I miss you, Mom.

Thanks for all the smiley faces.

Contents

Balance

Space

Foreword

When I'm tired or discouraged, or even when I'm feeling successful and maybe a little too full of myself, taking time to pay purposeful attention to God's hand and guidance grounds me. I love to examine the work he has done in my life. Actively looking for God's design of my days and my years gives me a peace that passes my finite understanding during moments of frustration or bewilderment over current circumstances. So many of my struggles are rooted in my tendency toward self-sufficiency and a desperate need to control my circumstances. But in the times when God rips these delusions from my tight-fisted grip, amazing things happen.

My career looks nothing like I dreamed or anything I planned, but it's so much more beautiful than what I would have designed.

I wanted to be a writer and assumed I'd write things about which I was confident. God had a different idea. He set me clearly (and begrudgingly) on the path of writing about the one thing I would have sworn I never could: organizing. Or more specifically: organizing as my personal ongoing struggle.

Though I resisted this direction for years, when I finally embraced God's design for my life, my family, my home, and my career, I was able to take a step back and see the beauty of his plan. God's design allows me to relax and be open and honest, and these are the core components of the personality he gave me. By accepting and eventually appreciating God's design, I have found my home in Christ and my place in the world.

I was so ready for Tracy's words in *A Redesigned Life*. Tracy's eye for design and her passion for beauty allow her to eloquently explain concepts in a way that I can apply to my life. Her formal training as an interior designer makes her the ideal teacher.

But most of all, Tracy has a passion to help those whom God has placed in her path. I'd known Tracy online for a few years before meeting her in person at a conference in 2017. I'm not even quite sure how it happened, but within minutes of recognizing one another, we were in prayer—the kind of prayer you long to experience with a heart friend. We prayed for this book, for the words you're about to read.

I've learned so much from Tracy. She explains principles of design as created by God (the original designer) and uses them to guide my understanding of how God works within my life. Movement, emphasis, pattern, contrast (and more) are not concepts I naturally understand, but as I learn them from Tracy, I also learn how to identify God's love, purpose, and design in the world and in me.

Be ready to understand yourself and your life more as you read *A Redesigned Life*. Whether you realize you're living in a "hallway season" or learn to embrace the beauty of space within your home and your heart, you'll be changed.

Dana K. White, ASlobComesClean.com (Reality-Based Cleaning and Organizing), author of *Decluttering at the Speed of Life* and *How to Manage Your Home Without Losing Your Mind*

Introduction

Everybody has their thing. Some are passionate about creating art, traveling the world, or major league baseball. I love decorating and anything beautiful that nourishes the soul. One of my "things" is looking at different colors and textures of fabric, which I realize is kind of weird.

But what I've come to notice is that fabric is rather blah when left on its rectangular cardboard bolt. Something happens to cream chenille or golden silk whenever a seamstress or designer grabs hold of it, cutting it from its cardboard bolt. As the designer cuts, arranges, and stitches portions of material together, the fabric is given shape and purpose. The same is true of us. Our lives are textiles in our divine Designer's hand.

Without him we're left on our own cardboard bolt—and, well . . . blah. God is not into blah. He's designed a specific set of plans for each of our lives using a set of principles. God cuts, arranges, stitches, and applies these principles, giving the fabric of our lives shape and purpose.

We go from blah to brilliant.

But sometimes we aren't feeling that brilliant, are we? To be honest, I don't always think a specific shape or purpose God designed for my life is all that flattering or beautiful. Life is turning out differently than I planned. And I bet the same is true for you too.

Maybe you are teaching algebra to a roomful of rowdy seventh graders when others promised you would make it as an actress. Perhaps you're grieving the loss of a friendship you assumed would always be there, or you're unpacking boxes in a place you swore you would never live. Or maybe you're thinking that you're supposed to be married by now, that you're supposed to weigh a certain amount so you can feel good about yourself, or that you're supposed to have more followers on social media. Maybe you think you should be a mother, or have a cancer-free body so you can watch your grandchildren grow.

I know women who are living through and wrestling with the things I just listed. This book is for them, and it's for you if parts of your life are not turning out the way you expected or hoped. All of us are living a life we did not design. So what do we do? And what about God? Where is he when life doesn't make sense? Together we'll explore these questions as we reconnect with God in the midst of our surprise or discouragement.

All of us are living a life we did not design.

The truth is, I'm living a life I didn't design but that God designed for me. I am me. A girl born and raised on the flat and humid plains of Kansas. I'm not a supermodel, celebrity, or accomplished athlete, and the world yawns at me.

But then . . . God. He is redesigning me.

Some seasons of my life are turning out as I had hoped. Other parts of my life surprise me in a hilariously awesome way, exceeding anything I could plan for or dream up myself. In fact, I'm supposed to be living in New York City making millions of dollars and owning my own interior design firm. But now I'm involved in women's ministry making way less than a million dollars.

From redesigning homes to redesigning hearts. From one kind of interior design to another kind. This is the essence of my story and why I am adding a designer's touch to the application of biblical teachings that will challenge and encourage you throughout the pages of this book. God is in the middle of every season of your life and is hand sewing your life into a one-of-a-kind, high-end couture masterpiece.

From blah to brilliant.

From obscure to couture.

God's movement in our lives is purposeful and perfectly timed. He's in the business of turning people who are discarded, misunderstood, and overlooked into accepted, known, and celebrated masterpieces.

Like a human interior designer or artist uses a set of design principles to help them create, God uses his own set of codes to create a couture life for each of us. Recognizing what these are is key to uncovering the purposes of God when life doesn't go as planned.

Let's consider six principles of design—God's use of **movement, emphasis, pattern, contrast, balance**, and **space**—and learn how these apply to you. These principles will enable us to uncover something spectacular about the purposes of our creative God.

In addition to these six principles, I've included design tips for your heart and home throughout this book to help you create beauty within and around you. Design is in the details. And good design is more than just picking a cute pillow or making sure the paint color complements the fabric on your couch. It's about using the elements and principles that make good design possible. Our God uses principles, so we should too.

But in the end, what truly makes a home beautiful is not the finishes or furnishings but the people who inhabit it. So create away, beautiful one, and settle in somewhere comfy.

Welcome home to your redesigned life.

I think you are about to be quite taken by its beauty.

DESIGN TIP
for Your Home and Heart

Set your minds on things above, not on earthly things.
(Col. 3:2)

While perusing Pinterest the other day, I stumbled upon a picture of my dream bedroom. It wasn't the furnishings that caught my attention. It was the ceiling, which was painted a pale blue color. Whoever designed this room "looked up" and saw the ceiling as an opportunity to add extra beauty to the room.

Don't forget to look up today—around your home and within your heart. Where is the focus of your heart? On earthly things or on the things of God? And what about your literal ceilings? Looking to spruce up a room in your home? Then add a pop of color to your ceiling. Remove some of those cobwebs from the corners, or the dust bunnies from your ceiling fan. Do not allow whatever is around you to take the focus off what is above you. Don't forget to look up.

Move

ment

one

Making God Your Focal Point

The older I get, the more I realize I have a lot of learning left to do. The world around me keeps changing. For example, I remember using a disposable camera with actual film in it to capture the moments and faces I didn't want to forget. I had to wait days to see if any of my pictures were any good. Appalling, isn't it?

I remember when MTV came out with something called a *music video*. Whoa. I even remember cursive handwriting and stores full of VHS tapes with movies on them. Heavens, I also recall getting my very first car phone. The thing came in a black leather bag that was about the same length as our bread box. It only worked while plugged in to my car's cigarette lighter, which was kind of a bummer. The thought that I would one day use this type of phone outside of my car and use it for pretty much everything *but* making phone calls in an emergency situation never crossed my Kirk Cameron–crushing adolescent brain.

But now we use our cell phones for multiple reasons and enjoy various social media apps like Instagram and Pinterest. We like these platforms because we are visual beings. All of us love to see and create pretty things, don't we? This is by design. God created us to be moved by what we see—to be drawn toward order and beauty. When we give in to our internal longing to create, organize, or "spruce things up," we are mimicking the creative attribute of God, whose image we bear.

Like Father, like daughter.

Imagine the towering Rocky Mountains, a fluorescent pink-and-purple sunset, or the wrinkled and smooshed face of a newborn baby. Grandness, brilliance, innocence. We are in awe of these things and moved by them because their beauty expresses parts of the divine nature of God.

We, the created, long to see glimpses of God, our Creator. The more we look for God, the more we will see him (Jer. 29:13). The more we see him, the more he becomes the focal point of our lives. And the more we focus on God, the more content and peaceful we become in the middle of life's surprises and detours.

God knows this. It's why God allows us to witness specific events or feel particular emotions that result from his movement in our lives, satisfying our need to understand the people and places we see. The

> The more we focus on God, the more content and peaceful we become in the middle of life's surprises and detours.

world around us will continue to change. But thankfully, we have a God who is in control and who helps us through this life whenever it doesn't go as we had planned. So let's uncover something about our God that you may not have realized and consider how the principle of movement causes him to become the focal point of your life.

Movement: Winding Lines, Shapes, and Curves

Movement is the principle of good design which gives the artist control over what the viewer sees next. Using this principle, the artist can create the path our eyes will travel as we look at a work of art. For example, our attention is first captured by the main focal point and then it proceeds to move around the composition as one element after another catches our attention.[1]

Speaking of your cell phone, if yours is nearby, ask Siri (or Alexa or Cortana or what's-her-name) to show you an image of the famous painting entitled *The Scream* by Edvard Munch. When I look at this painting, my focus lands immediately on the screaming figure's face. From there my eyes may move to the left and up the bridge to where I notice two other figures standing. Or my eyes may move to the right of the screaming figure and follow the river up and across the painting. From there my eyes travel back across the orange-and-yellow sky and down to the mysterious figures on the bridge, and then back to the screaming figure.

In *The Scream*, Munch used the design principle of movement to control what my eyes see as they move throughout the painting. He used curved brush strokes, straight lines, and color to guide my eyes around the painting. No matter which direction my eyes move, I always come back to the screaming figure, which is the intended focal point of the painting. Similarly, God directs what I see next as I move from one season of life to another. Like an artist in control of his painting, God is sovereign, or in complete control, over all of creation and over my life as well. God uses his own "principle of movement" so that no matter how many figurative bridges I travel across or orange-and-yellow skies I look upon, the eyes of my heart always come back to him, the focal point of my life. The specific ways God loves, stretches, heals, takes away, or gives are like the elements of curves, straight lines, and colors that artists use to catch our attention. All of these direct the eyes of our heart back to God as we move from one season of life to another.

Therefore, my dear brothers and sisters, stand firm. Let nothing move you. Always give yourselves fully to the work of the Lord, because you know that your labor in the Lord is not in vain. (1 Cor. 15:58)

In 1 Corinthians 15:58, the apostle Paul is saying that we do not need to look like the screaming figure in Edvard Munch's painting as we go through our days. But I bet that my children will tell you that on some days I do look like a screaming figure (more on that later).

I pray this book helps you stay steadfast and immovable in your faith whenever God's movement in your life surprises or challenges you. I long for us to stay close to the God who loves us whenever things do not go our way.

The world wobbles. Let's be people who stay steadfast and constant by focusing on the Person who *is* our constant. God's gracious and loving hands are persistent, sewing everything together for our good. Yes, the mending may hurt. Yes, the stitching may not make sense yet—or perhaps ever, this side of heaven. That's an uncomfortable reality I understand and am living. Yet God is worthy of our praise as our artistic Creator. He will use a figurative "straight line" of scriptural truth, or the "curve" of surprise, or the "edge" of rejection to move us to where we need to be for our greatest good and his greatest glory.

My friend Amy has experienced an "edge" of rejection that ultimately moved her closer to God. She is living her own redesigned life and, like the other ladies you will meet in the following chapters, is doing so beautifully. Here's what a broken heart and God's movement in Amy's life have taught her.

How My Shattered Heart Moved Me Closer to God

Amy Sullivan

Benji Halley was my sixth-grade crush. In math class, Benji shot rubber bands at me, and I was certain this was a sign of his undying love.

It was on the bus when Benji asked if I was going to the middle school dance, and on the bus where I managed to mumble an extended "ummmm" in response to his question. It was also on the bus that Benji said, "Well, I guess I'll see you there," and with a flip of his long, straight hair, he adjusted the volume on his Walkman, put on his headphones, and strutted down the aisle.

If twelve-year-old me knew anything, I knew this was love. It was the kind of love that made my heart beat out of my newly purchased, fake Guess sweatshirt.

But at the dance, I spent the night watching Benji talk to the popular girl who wore two Swatches. He didn't speak to me, and instead of my heart beating out of my sweatshirt, my heart felt as if it would shatter onto my white Keds.

That shattering was rejection, and even in sixth grade, I was a veteran when it came to rejection: my parents' divorce, yearly moves to new schools, new step-siblings, former step-siblings, the year I waited for the coveted invite to the cool girls' table, and of course, all the times in PE when I was chosen last or not at all.

I couldn't wait to grow up because I was certain adults never dealt with this kind of rejection.

But time passed, and no longer was I rejected by a long-haired boy in a dark gym. Instead, rejection happened out in the open for the world to see. Rejection was when the ring fit the finger of another girl, the baby went to the couple who already had three children, and the job was awarded to someone more qualified. Regardless, rejection still felt as if my heart would shatter and fall onto my shoes.

But what twelve-year-old me never knew and adult me tends to forget is that even through life's nos, God still moves.

I scheme and flail, desperate for my prayers to be answered. I beg God to help me avoid pain and loss. I call out for him to use me or answer my questions. I rationalize that what I ask for is reasonable and good. I focus on what I need as opposed to who he is, and I forget. I forget God tells people no, and he tells them no often.

God told Moses no when he wanted to enter the Promised Land (Deut. 3:25–26).

God told Elijah no when he prayed God would take his life (1 Kings 19:4–8).

And God tells me no (daily).

The uncomfortable edge of no isn't God's rejection, it's his plan to move me to a different place, a place that may not look as I envisioned, but a place closer to him.

As Amy shared in her story, God has a loving purpose for each of us and is using things like rejection from boys named Benji to move us closer to him. However, when hard and hurtful things happen to us, it doesn't always feel like God loves us. Know this: our God does not support or create whatever evil comes into our lives. The Bible teaches that Satan and mankind itself take what God creates and use it for evil (Mic. 2:1; John 10:10; Rom. 3:10–18; 1 Pet. 5:8). Can God use evil and pain for something good and useful? Yes (Gen. 50:20). But God is never the source of evil, nor does God delight in it or tempt us to do evil things (Ps. 5:4; Job 34:10; James 1:13).

Movement within the Pages of Scripture

Okay, I need to confess something before we go further. I like to ponder. My mind never stops. I am not sure why, but I have a theory. Brace yourself.

Once upon a time, my mother let me crawl around in the dirt at my dad's softball games and eat cigarette butts that littered the ground. Oh yes, 'tis true. Why she felt the need to share this hideous story with me and find it hilarious, I will never know. But the bigger issue is that as a wee tot, I ate used cigarette butts while in my mother's presence.

It was the 1970s. Moms did not have hand-sanitizer bottles clipped to their diaper bags, and they must have figured that babies had immune systems or something. I do not know. I am still appalled by this truth from my childhood. I am convinced recycled nicotine accumulating in the tissues of my young, absorbent brain made me hyper-wired for pondering.

So . . . surprise! I've been thinking and I want you to join me in doing the same, but as it pertains to your own life. God has a set of plans he designed with your name written all over them. And the way he carries out his plans for your life is purposeful and providential.

God's Providence

The providence of God means the continuing action of God in preserving his creation and guiding it toward his intended purposes. . . . It means that we are able to live in the assurance that God is present and active in our lives. We are in his care and can therefore face the future confidently, knowing that things are not happening merely by chance.[2]

God is with us and involved in our lives. This is why we can confidently and even joyfully live out a life we did not design. Each of the design principles mentioned in this book refers back to what theologians call God's providence. In fact, the word *providence* comes from a Latin term that means "to foresee."[3] This concept is a pivotal one.

God's providence means that he knows the future because he already designed it. God's movement in our lives is not random. He prepares and matures us, readying us to receive what he's already planned. If we miss this, we will wobble. The life we're living will seem like a continuous game of roulette, making us feel nervous, depressed, or queasy. Yes, a rush of adrenaline comes with playing the real game of roulette. But I don't want to live on adrenaline; I want to live on *assurance*.

Whether life surprises us in a wonderful or painful way, we can know that what is happening is part of God's movement. God did not create the world and then leave it. God doesn't play roulette with our lives. What he has planned will come to pass, for he said it would (Num. 23:19; Isa. 46:9–11). This

What he has planned will come to pass. . . . This is not assurance based on impersonal odds, but assurance based on one personal God.

is not assurance based on impersonal odds, but assurance based on one personal God.

What Providence Means

Several verses in Scripture support the assurances I mentioned and teach that God is moving and is intimately involved in our lives. This is wonderful news! Here's why:

God is unstoppable.

"I have revealed and saved and proclaimed—
I, and not some foreign god among you.
You are my witnesses," declares the LORD, "that
I am God.
Yes, and from ancient days I am he.
No one can deliver out of my hand.
When I act, who can reverse it?" (Isa. 43:12–13)

God is eternal.

But the plans of the LORD stand firm forever,
the purposes of his heart through all generations.
(Ps. 33:11)

God is righteous.

So listen to me, you men of understanding.
Far be it from God to do evil,
from the Almighty to do wrong. (Job 34:10)

God is holding everything together.

For in him all things were created: things in heaven and on earth, visible and invisible, whether thrones or powers or rulers or authorities; all things have been created through him and for him. He is before all things, and in him all things hold together. (Col. 1:16–17)

Scripture is full of additional verses like these that prove God is present in our lives and he cares for his creation. God is omniscient or all-knowing. He knows what he is doing. It's up to us whether we live on our adrenaline or on his assurances. Adrenaline leads to wobbliness. Assurance leads to steadfastness. It is one or the other.

So don't give in to discouragement. God uses the principle of movement to bring himself into focus so you can see him more clearly and love him more fully. May we remain steadfast in our faith with our eyes ever fixed on God when life doesn't go as planned.

two

Staying Steadfast When Dreams Die

When I was five years old, I accompanied my mother to see *The Nutcracker* ballet. I loved watching the brave sprite Nutcracker battle it out with the crusty old Mouse King. However, my favorite character was the Sugar Plum Fairy. She was beautiful. Her pink tutu sparkled under the lights as she twirled around the stage. Wide eyed, I looked into my mother's face and said, "I am going to be her one day."

I kid you not, from the ages of five to eighteen I believed that my sole purpose in life was to be the Sugar Plum Fairy. While other peers experienced sports, band, and the world known as "teen dating," I was at the dance studio stretching and pirouetting away. I entered my senior year of high school confident the coveted part was mine. I tried out for the part but never danced in the role of the Sugar Plum Fairy. I was devastated, but my parents encouraged me to dance the part I was given to the best of my ability. So I did.

A couple of weeks after my last *Nutcracker* performance, I received a card in the mail from a lady who I did not know and still, to my knowledge, have never met. Here is a portion of what it said:

> *Dearest Tracy, a little bird told me that you were not chosen to dance the part of the Sugar Plum Fairy and that it stung your heart and pierced your eyes with tears. I watched you rise above your tears and discouragement. I want you to know that you danced splendidly in the part God chose just for you. You have given me the courage to face my own fear of discouragement and to go for my dreams. You have given me a* Nutcracker *memory that I will cherish forever . . .*

I just stared at the card in my hand. Someone noticed me even though I was not dancing in a lead role. Someone heard about my disappointment and cared. Then there were these words:

The part God chose just for you . . .

God chose . . .

These words have stuck in my heart since 1993. They have changed my life. God has changed my life. I didn't really know him back then in a personal way. Who was this God and what could he possibly want with my life if I was not going to become a prima ballerina?

As I write these words to you today, I am resting in the fact that it was never God's plan for me to wear a pink tutu. His role for me involved ministering to a discouraged and fearful woman. This was God's part for me. Sure, having my name in the program, a bouquet of roses, and applause would have been wonderful. But programs tear and are thrown away. Roses die. Earthly glory fades. Yet the words in a letter given to me decades ago remain.

You, yes YOU, are dancing splendidly in the part God chose just for you.

God chooses specific parts for *all* of us to play. Yes, they may involve a figurative pink tutu and place us in the spotlight. But more than likely, we find ourselves in a plain leotard under fluorescent lighting. And we all know the number fluorescent lighting pulls on our complexion. Give me natural lighting, please. And let me wear a sweatshirt and yoga pants. Leotards are not forgiving.

It is either God's way or my way. My name in lights or his name written on my heart. Only one of us deserves center stage in my heart, and though God will never force me to give it to him, I willingly offer it to him now.

Why? Because God sent his Son, Jesus, to be rejected, crucified, and resurrected for this messy, obscure, and imperfect woman. Jesus conquered death so I can stand before God completely forgiven and loved. I no longer need to be center stage. Center stage is just a location and not my salvation.

God's movement through the loss of a dream started to reveal the real focus and direction my life was about to take. I still step onto stages from time to time. I do so now not as a ballerina but as a Bible teacher. From teaching pirouettes to teaching the biblical book of Proverbs. From teaching tondus to teaching theology. Thankfully, I no longer have to wear a leotard, and my toes look a lot better these days.

Remaining Steadfast Despite Her Past

In the Gospel of Luke we're introduced to an unnamed woman who did something pretty radical at the feet of Jesus. I wonder if this woman ever dreamed of being a wife, adored and cherished by her husband for the rest of her days. Perhaps she imagined cradling her newborn and singing into its tiny ears as it lay in her arms. While Scripture is silent on this woman and her upbringing, I think it's safe to assume at some point messages of motherhood and marriage were probably spoken into her heart. Historians note that back in Jesus's day, Jewish women didn't hold jobs outside of the home.

As in the pagan cultures, the family was of utmost importance for the Hebrew woman. According to rabbinic sources, they regarded age 12 as the suitable age for Jewish girls to be given in marriage. In the rabbinic ideal, women are not to be found in the marketplace, where the risk to their chastity was considered enormous.[1]

Judaism in the first century had emerged from the oriental patriarchal tradition in which women were considered the property of men with no rights, no role in society except childbearing, and no education.[2]

And here she was, in the marketplace, working as a prostitute. Known by many men, loved and cherished by none of them. Excluded instead of included. Dismissed instead of welcomed. Judged instead of loved. A prostitute instead of a wife and mother. Then she encountered Jesus.

Now this woman was no longer hiding. She was out in the open and right in the middle of a dinner party that she was not invited to. Luke records that this woman did not invite herself over to sell her body to a man. No, she came to the party to offer adoration to her Lord.

> When one of the Pharisees invited Jesus to have dinner with him, he went to the Pharisee's house and reclined at the table. A woman in that town who lived a sinful life learned that Jesus was eating at the Pharisee's house, so she came there with an alabaster jar of perfume. As she stood behind him at his feet weeping, she began to wet his feet with her tears. Then she wiped them with her hair, kissed them and poured perfume on them. (Luke 7:36–38)

What brought this woman from a darkened alley and into the room where Jesus sat? Scripture is silent. Something happened to her. God's movement taught this woman she mattered and that God had a new part and overarching purpose for her life. Yes, she needed to repent of her lifestyle, but Jesus was the focal point of her life. This woman gave all she had, her reputation and her valuable perfumed ointment, to worship Jesus and anoint his feet. Her sacrifice socially and materially proved her newfound commitment to Jesus. And her redesigned life has now been acknowledged within the pages of our Bibles and celebrated throughout human history.

> Then [Jesus] turned toward the woman and said to Simon, "Do you see this woman? I came into your house. You did not give me any water for my feet, but she wet my feet with her tears and wiped them with her hair. You did not give me a kiss, but this woman, from the time I entered, has not stopped kissing my feet. You did not put oil on my head, but she has poured perfume on my feet. Therefore, I tell you, her many sins have

been forgiven—as her great love has shown. But whoever has been forgiven little loves little." (Luke 7:44–47)

Sadly, the unnamed woman had her critics. And Jesus was willing to stand up to one of them on her behalf. He asked Simon, "Do you see this woman?"

Do you see *her*, Simon?

Not do you see what she is *known for*. Or do you see what she *has done*, but do you *see her*—a person made in my image? How beautiful is this? Jesus sees past our current role or the parts we played when we were younger. He sees past our makeup and edited social media posts. God in the flesh sees you and he sees me—people made in his image or likeness (Gen. 1:26–27). We are known by him and loved by him because we are his.

Then Jesus said to her, "Your sins are forgiven."

The other guests began to say among themselves, "Who is this who even forgives sins?"

Jesus said to the woman, "Your faith has saved you; go in peace." (Luke 7: 48–50)

In the middle of dinner, something beautiful had just taken place. A woman who was considered filthy was set free and forgiven. Yet the onlookers questioned and grumbled among themselves. Why did they miss the point?

We can look at what is happening and continue to grumble and question. We too may have missed the point. Don't miss it anymore. We can continue to long after our own purposes or plans, or we can come before our God and pour out all of who we are before him.

And here is the beautiful thing. *Jesus sees you.*

Whenever you and I worship him, surrender our lives to Jesus, or weep over and repent of our sin, we will never be turned away. First John 1:9 promises that God is faithful to forgive and cleanse us of our sins.

We have been forgiven much. May it be said of us that we love like this woman, giving all that we have to Jesus.

The world will probably not remember us in the way it remembers this woman. But God remembers every tear we shed. Every "I love you, Lord" we utter. He sees and remembers all. God is redesigning our lives to align with the purposes he has planned for us. There are no small parts in God's plans for our lives. Center stage is just a location and not our salvation.

Center stage is just a location and not our salvation.

We may want to live a certain way or have a certain something. But God is providential and may plan something different for a particular season of our life. Why? Because he knows where all of us are headed. This life and this world as we see it now isn't our destination. So let's remain steadfast in our faith despite our past or despite the accusations of others. God is moving and he is providential.

Prostitute to worshiper. Judged to forgiven. Unloved to beloved. Brought from obscurity to known for all eternity. This is one woman's story, and it is our story too.

Staying Steadfast When God Uses Movement in Your Life

I am sure you have had a dream die, or have felt unloved or judged for reasons that left you reeling. My friend Catherine can relate. Here is what she does whenever her faith feels wobbly:

Is life easy and pain-free? Hardly. Sometimes, life is so difficult and gut-wrenchingly painful that I can no longer stand. But in those moments when I doubt my self-worth and purpose, wondering, "When will you use me, Lord?" I kneel and ask God to remind me of his purpose and that my identity rests firmly and steadfastly in him.

When the enemy whispers lies of my smallness and lack of self-worth, God's presence proves again and again that I am more precious than priceless jewels. Every colored hair on my head was planned with loving purpose and intent. My shape, my smile, my personality—all the quirky traits that make me who I am—were crafted by a loving God.

And you know what? Whatever your circumstance, no matter the struggles you may face or the joys you may celebrate, you are living the life God designed just for you with a loving purpose. Only you. No one else fits the design crafted especially for you, and God did that on purpose. For you. Because you are loved.

~Catherine Bird

Like Catherine, we can either focus on our problem or on God's providence and our identity in him. In order to do so and remain steadfast whenever life leaves you wobbly, make these practices a priority:

- *Meet with God.* Focus on who he is and pour out all your frustration, anger, anxiety, or sorrow before him. Pray and pray some more. Ask God to help your unbelief and to help you remain faithful to what he has designed for you (Mark 9:24). Ask God to remind you of how he sees you and to assure you that you are secure and significant because you are his beloved child.

- *Keep a record of God's movement in your life.* Write down the specifics of seasons filled with rejection, loss, or failure. Make note of what you learned about God and yourself as you walked through them. Looking back on these moments helps you find the strength and assurance to trust God again the next time you feel wobbly.

- *Let go of the need to control and understand.* Release control of your life along with the need to figure everything out or make life fair and pain-free. You and I are not God but are divinely designed by him to be human. Even though God has given us the capacity to feel anger, vengeance is God's arena (Rom. 12:19). He will return to the earth and make all things right (Rev. 20:11–13). So ask God to help you surrender your life to him and help you be at peace whenever justice seems impossible or answers escape you.

- *Move forward.* Each day is new and full of God's mercies (Lam. 3:22–24). Trust that God knows what he is doing because he is eternal, righteous, unstoppable, and in control. If you are stuck in the past you cannot remain steadfast in the present. Make God the focal point of your life by fixating upon *him*. Doing so enables you to live on assurance instead of adrenaline.

> You will keep in perfect peace
>   all who trust in you,
>   all whose thoughts are fixed on you!
> Trust in the LORD always,
>   for the LORD GOD is the eternal Rock. (Isa. 26:3–4
>   NLT)

Do not give in to discouragement. God is using movement to set the direction of your life and to bring him into focus so you can see him more clearly. God will not compete with our plans. So he places winding lines, shapes, and edges throughout his designs for your life.

Watch for God's movement and learn from it; it is purposeful and perfectly timed. Dance splendidly in the part he has chosen just for you. You'll find that once the reality of God comes into focus, things such as your purpose become clearer.

God is using movement to set the direction of your life and to bring him into focus so you can see him more clearly. God will not compete with our plans.

Muse Minutes

Ever heard of a muse? A *muse* is something or someone that inspires or motivates us to create or reflect. Many things inspire and motivate me. Sunsets, various paintings, classical music, and pieces of literature cause me to think and ponder. What inspires you? As Christians, God should be our ultimate Muse. But it is hard to focus on him amid the distractions of this world. So I want to help you refocus on God and his purposes in your life. I encourage you to take the next few minutes and work through the following section. Grab a pen and record your answers in the space that follows. No rush. Pray, ponder, enjoy this time with your heavenly Designer.

1. To help cement principle #1 into that beautiful mind and heart of yours, rewrite in your own words what *movement* is here.

   Rewrite in your own words how God uses this principle in our lives.

2. What is the focal point of your life? If you asked a friend, family member, or neighbor what the focal point of your life is, what do you think their response would be and why? And if the answer to these questions was not God, what may be preventing this from happening?

3. How can you remain steadfast in your faith when you face life's trials, surprises, or disappointments?

DESIGN TIP
for Your Home and Heart

There is a time for everything,
and a season for every activity under the heavens.
(Eccles. 3:1)

Not much thought or design effort is given to the hallways in our homes. We may choose a railing for the stairs or wooden trim for the bottom and top of the walls that flank the hallway spaces in our homes. But avoid putting too many things along the walls of your hallways since these spaces are usually narrower and exist to help you move from one living space of your home to another.

Metaphorically speaking, I believe that a good number of us are in a "hallway" type season of life. We don't feel like celebrating a hallway season because it appears empty. We find ourselves figuratively surrounded by blank, bare walls. Our hearts long to fill those walls with the same trophies or pictures that hang on other people's walls.

God is helping me see that hallway seasons deserve to be celebrated and acknowledged. A blank space allows us time to prepare for the future hanging of pictures we have yet to take. Bare walls enable us to breathe and love those around us more deeply.

Be encouraged. Celebrate your hallway. It's a beautiful place to be too.

Emp

hasis

three

Living Out Your Pop of Color for God

I remember thinking that Luke Skywalker was a hunk the first time I watched *Star Wars*. I adored his puppy dog eyes and feathered hair. Life had been hard for poor Luke. I felt bad for him because he was stuck fixing robots on an uncool planet with a bizarre name. But as we all know, this was not to be Luke's ultimate destiny. His destiny was to become a Jedi and use the Force to overcome the Dark Side and help the Rebel forces defeat the Empire.

With the help of the master Jedi, Yoda, Luke was able to accept his new destiny, train for it, and resist the temptation of the Dark Side. The emphasis of Luke's life changed. Yoda set before Luke the option of choosing the light or the darkness. The same choice is before us as Christians: to obey and love God or deny him and give in to the darkness of sin within us. There is a battle that is raging within us and around us. We must engage in it as Luke Skywalker did.

Whether we wield a lightsaber or a laptop, God is moving all of us toward the main emphasis of our lives, which is ultimately glorifying him. This is by design. God will open certain doors and close other doors in order to make the specifics of our emphasis evident. As we are about to see, fellow Padawan, if there is ill-placed emphasis in your life or in mine, we will not be able to enjoy and effectively live a life we did not design.

Emphasis: Bringing Attention to What Is Important

Emphasis creates a focal point in a design which brings attention to the element or area that is most important. . . .

If everything is emphasized (all the text is large and bold, all the images are animated, everything is in bright colors) nothing will stand out, and grab the viewer's attention. If everything is emphasized, nothing is.[1]

I love simple and elegant design. We've all seen pictures of a living room with its crisp white walls and cream sofa. Imagine a coffee table in the middle of that living room. On top of the table sits a glass vase filled with a bouquet of orange tulips or powder blue hydrangeas. Or perhaps there is a turquoise-and-white paisley pattern rug under the coffee table. Maybe there is a large abstract oil painting hanging on the wall composed of green, blue, and purple horizontal stripes. Our eyes are drawn to the flowers, to the rug, or to the oil painting because of the pop of color they provide among all the white. This is the essence of emphasis as a design principle. Emphasis makes us stop, helping us focus. A designer uses shapes, texture, or color to create emphasis.

Imagine the same living room but now everything in it is red—from the couch to the walls to the flowers to the rug. I don't want to linger or enjoy the space because it's overwhelming and nothing grabs my attention. There's too much red. Nothing is emphasized.

In the same way, our world is pressing us to be like an all-red room. We must be all things to all people all the time, it seems. Good at everything. Involved in everything. Know everyone. I'm tired of the pressure, of all the striving, competition, and backbiting. Give me some white space, please. I need God to give me emphasis and so do you.

Our little pops of color should cause others to rest the eyes of their hearts and minds upon God.

God is not asking us to be all things to all people all the time. He's the one who is capable of doing and being this. He's the one who is all-knowing. God alone is our ever-present help and shield. We're only to add our little pop of color into the corner of the world in which he places us. We do this through the emphasis that God has designed for each of us. The beautiful thing is, all our emphases or callings will look different. However different they may be, our little pops of color should cause others to rest the eyes of their hearts and minds upon God. And if we are doing too many things, we will be way too red or stressed out; our dark side will surface, fellow Padawan, and no one will want to linger around us either.

My friend Katie knows all too well the danger of all-red-room thinking. Here's what happened when she tried to live this way and what happened when she actually lived in an all-red room in her house.

Increasing the White Space in Your Life

— Katie Reid —

When we moved into our house, the master bedroom was painted red—as in, all four walls boasted crimson. Granted, this was ten years prior to the white-room craze, but even then, the top-to-bottom semi-gloss made quite a statement. The bedroom was fairly large, with two floor-length windows. It exuded romance; I liked it.

At first the color felt sophisticated—a complementary backdrop to our swirling black-and-white comforter and throw pillows. But over time the all-red room became cumbersome—almost cave-like when Michigan's gray skies hid the sun.

If three of the bedroom walls had been painted a soft color and just one of the walls had been bold, the ambiance would have been more appealing. But surrounded by red, my eyes longed for a focal point instead of a bombardment of color.

My Instagram feed used to mimic our master bedroom. It was full of bright images with little white space. It was hard to take in the depth of what was there due to the onslaught of vivid tones. So I started breaking up the busyness with some intentional blocks of calm . . . and not just on my Instagram feed, but in my off-screen life too.

As a woman who likes to get things done, I sometimes overdo it. I say yes too often, and pretty soon my to-do list morphs into all-red walls with little white space. When your eyes have no place to land, when you forfeit rest, and when you insist on trying to do it all, body-and-soul fatigue sets in. But when you place boundaries to guide your eyes toward your focal point, breathing room is created.

I'm designed to be a doer, but that is not a license to live in a constant state of overwhelm. In fact, when I push too hard, I end up depleted physically and emotionally. A couple of times my lack of restraint has landed me in bed for the day—thoroughly exhausted from pushing the limits and doing too much. God has used these instances to reset my priorities, to hone my focus so as not to cloud my vision.

All-red living can seem exciting at first, but it is not sustainable for the long run. Saturating our schedules proves cumbersome— almost claustrophobic.

As a singer, speaker, writer, and photographer, I realized something had to give. My well-laid plans required alteration if I was going to remain standing. I was entering an intense writing season, and even though I was good at photography, it needed to take a back seat. It was a hard but necessary decision. I referred my clients to other photographers so I could be more productive in another area.

A beautiful by-product of eliminating some of the noise from my schedule was that it created room for others to step up and step into their giftings. Since I was no longer trying to do it all, there was space for others at the table. Although it didn't feel natural to change course, my soul could breathe more fully when I stopped living all-red.

Emphasis within the Pages of Scripture

Like Katie, I too have found more room to breathe as a result of cutting down on the number of commitments I say yes to. I'm tired of striving and pushing myself to the limit, and perhaps you are too. If we're not careful we can become busy listening to ourselves rather than allowing God to reveal our emphasis. How can we walk with God and know what ours is? The key to discovering and living out our emphasis is found in sanctification; this is what helps us produce pops of color for the glory of our God.

God's Role in Sanctification

One theologian defines sanctification as "a progressive work of God and man that makes us more and more free from sin and like Christ in our actual lives."[2] The Bible teaches that once a person has asked for forgiveness and received Jesus Christ as their Savior by faith, the Holy Spirit indwells them, saving them from eternal separation from God (John 3:16; 16:7–14; Eph. 2:8–10; 1 John 1:9). The Holy Spirit changes or transforms a saved Christian "from one degree of glory to another," helping them think and act in ways that bring honor and glory to God, which is the essence of sanctification (2 Cor. 3:18 ESV; Gal. 5:22–23; 2 Thess. 2:13).

How God specifically works within each of our lives varies. But there are ways we can see he is up to some sanctifying work in our lives when:

God disciplines.

> My son, do not make light of the Lord's discipline,
>   and do not lose heart when he rebukes you,
> because the Lord disciplines the one he loves,
>   and he chastens everyone he accepts as his son.
> (Heb. 12:5–6)

God leads.

For those who are led by the Spirit of God are the children of God. (Rom. 8:14)

God empowers.

For it is God who works in you to will and to act in order to fulfill his good purpose. (Phil. 2:13)

God changes our desires.

Therefore, if anyone is in Christ, the new creation has come: The old has gone, the new is here! (2 Cor. 5:17)

Our Part in Sanctification

It may seem like sanctification is carried out only by the Holy Spirit, and it mostly is. We play a passive role in one sense as we rely on the Spirit and trust him to transform us, no matter how many times we mess up (Rom. 6:13–14; 12:1). But we also play an active role in our sanctification as we seek to obey God and become more like him, carrying out the plans he has designed for our life (Rom. 12:2; Eph. 2:10; James 1:22–24).

The apostle Paul exhorts you and me to take responsibility for how we think and act. He writes that we are to "work out" our faith and the privileges that come with our salvation with "fear and trembling" while God works in and with us, helping us to accomplish his designs for our lives (Phil. 2:12–13).

I am tired of the world telling us we can have and do whatever we want whenever we want to do it. This is all-red-room thinking and not what God is saying. Beware. "Whatever and whenever" is not wise. But God is wise, so trust him as he transforms you. The more we allow the Holy Spirit to sanctify us, the more we will grow in holiness and in our ability to discern our emphasis.

Looking at God's No from a Different Perspective

But what if we really feel like we found our calling or purpose, and then it doesn't happen? Sometimes the emphasis we wish for or desire in our hearts will not come to pass because God will say no and not allow it to happen. We may assume this is because God is not good or fair. Or maybe we believe we are not good enough for God to use us, or that God doesn't care about the dreams or passions that we feel inside us. But this isn't true.

Look at God's no from a different perspective. God, because he is good and is in the process of sanctifying us, could be saying no to our good desires simply because they are not in line with the emphasis he has designed for our overall life. And God's no enables our pop of color to be a beneficial and beautiful one. Here it is in a nutshell:

> God's no = not our emphasis.
>
> God's no = the revealing of his emphasis for us.
>
> God's no = his protection, preventing us from becoming an all-red room.

When God says no, that means we will have the opportunity to say yes to something that he has decided is better for us, because in his providence he knows and has already designed what is to come.

And when God says no, that means we will have the opportunity to say yes to something that he has decided is better for us, because in his providence he knows and has already designed what is to come.

Allowing the Pinch of the Holy Spirit to Help You Pop

I'm not going to mince words. I am a slightly extroverted woman who loves people. Like, *loves* people. I initially tried to extinguish my love for writing, because I pictured all writers as wool-sweater-wearing types that live in secluded cabins in the woods. I don't wear wool. I need to talk and give hugs. And no to lots of nature, but I will take a beach. In fact, my family and I recently returned from a Caribbean cruise, or "extrovert heaven" as I like to call cruises. Lots of happy people stuck on a boat together out at sea. Yep, sign me up, because cruise = lots of talking just waiting to happen.

One evening on the way to dinner, I saw two women huddled around what I call the "claw game." Pay a couple bucks, maneuver a mechanical claw, try to grab a prize—in this case, a stack of money—and drop it down the chute to win. I have never seen anyone win the claw game, so I felt pity for these poor souls and stopped to watch, assuming this would result in no one winning anything and provide another opportunity for me to commiserate with complete strangers because #extroverthabit.

But this woman operated the claw like a boss and was able to grab a stack of one-hundred-dollar bills, drop them into the chute, and win! We high-fived and I was filled with, like, pure . . . joy. Stop thinking I am weird. This lady was amazing.

Sanctification can kind of seem like a claw too if we do not understand it and instead choose to fight it. We sometimes act like one of those prizes in the claw game. We become content to lie in what we assume is a safe, glass cage, in a pile with everyone else. But then we feel the pinch of the Spirit's conviction, exhortation, or discipline, and so we shimmy away from it. Don't! That pinch is God's loving way of pulling us away from ease or from what everyone else in the proverbial pile is doing. You know what I am talking about. Anyone else needing a cruise right now?

> It is for freedom that Christ has set us free. Stand firm, then, and do not let yourselves be burdened again by a yoke of slavery. (Gal. 5:1)

Let God grab you and lift you out of the pile. Jesus laid himself upon the cross so you and I wouldn't be confined to living life in any sort of cage. You are designed to be different, holy, set apart from the mundane. God pinches so you can pop! Sanctification, then, is the emphasis-making process that God uses to grow, stretch, and mature you, and to reveal the specifics of the calling he has designed just for you.

The more you cooperate with the process of sanctification, the more your efforts to live a life of holiness will pay off. God promises that you will experience more joy and peace as you allow him to change you "from one degree of glory to another" (2 Cor. 3:18 ESV; Gal. 5:22–23; Rom. 14:17).

> May God himself, the God of peace, sanctify you through and through. May your whole spirit, soul and body be kept blameless at the coming of our Lord Jesus Christ. (1 Thess. 5:23)

I want you to find contentment and win in life in ways that truly matter. So don't

Jesus laid himself upon the cross so you and I wouldn't be confined to living life in any sort of cage. You are designed to be different, holy, set apart from the mundane.

try to be all things or do all things. God uses the principle of emphasis to sanctify you and to protect you from burning out. May we submit to God's pinch whenever life doesn't go as planned and pop when necessary so others can be blessed and God can be further glorified.

Oh, and if an extrovert comes up to you either on land or at sea, please have mercy on her. Give her a hug or a high-five. You'll make her day. I pinkie swear it.

four

Knowing When to Say Yes or No

After I determined my sole purpose in life was not to be the Sugar Plum Fairy, I explored another world that piqued my interest—the world of interior design. I watched the winsome Delta Burke on the TV show *Designing Women* back in the late 1980s. Working at Sugarbaker & Associates seemed like a fabulous gig. The TV characters seemed to just sit and talk on luxurious couches all day long. Yep, sign me up. I wanted to be an interior designer.

So off I went to Kansas State University, declaring interior design as my major. Over the next four years I learned that real designers do not sit on couches and talk all day long. They work hard. And I worked hard, building foamcore models and sketching countless floorplans.

By the time my senior year of college rolled around, I had the rest of my life figured out. My plan was to graduate and move to New York City and own my own design firm. Make millions of dollars. Drive a Mercedes and carry a Prada purse on my arm. Have a ten-foot waterfall wall encircled by a reflecting pond in the middle of my living room. My little twentysomething brain seriously concluded that the rest of my days were going to be filled with these things and with colorful fabric swatches.

Somewhere in between watching reruns of O.J. Simpson fleeing the police on a California freeway and the court case that followed, I designed the life I wanted to live. In May of 1998, I graduated with a BS in interior design. I eventually connected with a design firm in Phoenix, Arizona, and moved there the following July.

Over the next year, I dived into the fundamental teachings of my faith. I attended my first Bible study and met my first Christian friend. This same friend encouraged me to join her in serving the youth at our church. I flat out laughed at her. Youth ministry? This meant I'd have to see and be around teenagers. No way, not me. Not going to happen. But my friend persisted, so I ended up with a group of teenage girls to mentor. As the years passed and more teen girls came into my life, I tried to ignore God's calling, but he wouldn't let me. God had a different kind of interior design for me to do.

The first group of teenage girls I mentored were younger versions of me. As I looked into their faces and listened to their doubts and fears, my heart broke. No one had taught my teenage heart about Jesus either. I realized that this was a chance for me to help my girls learn about the one Person who alone defines, fulfills, and loves perfectly and eternally. True beauty and significance is found in Jesus Christ alone. It's not in fashionable products, position, power, or people's opinions. How I wanted my girls to grasp this. To live this.

So I poured myself into the lives of these girls, teaching them the biblical truths most precious to me. To my amazement, they actually listened, except for when a cute boy walked by. So of course our Bible study chats would usually end up focusing on boys, but I do believe they caught something about Jesus along the way.

I was happily designing offices during the day, discussing plausible prom dresses at night, and playing paintball on the weekend at youth retreats. Eventually I was asked to consider serving as an intern for the youth ministry at my church. Why me? I felt like an underdog when it came to anything ministry related, and there was this small issue of me being a woman. Men served in the majority of the paid leadership positions in our church. But my gender and lack of biblical knowledge were never an issue with God. Every excuse I offered him was lovingly ignored. So I started interning and also enrolled in seminary.

Now this is straight up hilarious.

I went to a secular school and not a Bible college to study interior design. But I soon found myself shoulder deep in hermeneutics, theological doctrines, and the writings of Josephus. To say I was overwhelmed and feeling inferior as I studied beside seasoned male pastors is an understatement. Two years later, I graduated and was hired by my church to be their full-time director of student women.

As the years passed, I trained and shepherded the volunteer staff of women, and organized and led mission trips and purity conferences. I held broken young women as they disclosed their struggles with their sexual purity, eating disorders, depression, suicidal thoughts, drug addiction, and self-harm. I cried with one of my girls as she handed her newborn daughter over to the adoption agency. I heard and saw the effects of rape and divorce, and held the hand of a weeping student as we buried her classmate.

These are what I call "holy moments" that I will carry with me forever. These are the moments when I witnessed God's presence trump the collision of faith and circumstance. Over and over God moved, changed, healed, comforted, and restored. To watch this happen in the lives of his children captivates me and leaves me speechless.

Who am I that the Lord would allow me to love even one of his children? I've learned that my arms are not here to hold Prada purses. My arms are here to hold the hurting.

From loving on-trend paint colors to loving on people.

From one kind of interior design to another.

I was now a woman in ministry.

When God Said No to King David

Following God is not always easy nor is it dull. You may, however, find some comfort in remembering that God said no to his sons and daughters throughout Scripture as well. Even King David, who was probably a killer paintball player (just ask Goliath) and loved God with his whole heart, heard a no from God in regard to something he wanted to do for God. In his own way, David set his eye on a different kind of Prada purse that was of great value and worth. The mighty king wanted to build a temple for God, whom he loved. But this was not in the plans that God had designed for his life. So God said no to David.

David's Pops of Color

Thank goodness for King David. The psalms that he penned encourage and comfort my heart. If I'm feeling frustrated or scared I turn to Psalm 23 or Psalm 91. When I find myself growing impatient or feeling down, I run to the words that David wrote in Psalm 27 and Psalm 42. I am a Psalms groupie. I cannot get enough of them.

The Psalms are one of David's pops of color. He was also a shepherd, a great military victor, and king of Israel—all pops of color that went along with God's movement in David's life, aligning him with his emphases. But there was one thing David desired to do that would have put him over into the too-much-red-in-one-room category.

To be fair, I want to show David some grace, and not just because I'm his groupie. He was the king. He clearly worshiped God and desired for the rest of Israel to follow his lead. And yet according to 1 Kings 3:2–4, all of Israel was worshiping and sacrificing to God on "high places," or altars that were located on lofty and visible places.

I believe we can worship or love God from wherever we are, but high places were often used for the worship of false gods. Perhaps David was bothered by this, but what 2 Samuel 7:2 says is that David saw how he himself was dwelling in a "house of cedar, while the ark of God remains in a tent."

So I don't fault David for wanting to build a temple that could provide a place for God to be worshiped in ways befitting and honoring his holiness. When David told Nathan the prophet his plan, his advisor gave him a thumbs-up. So things were looking up for David. He had the heart, the resources, and the support of a good and godly buddy to proceed with building a temple for God.

And then God intervened.

> Go and tell my servant David, "This is what the LORD says: Are you the one to build me a house to dwell in? I have not dwelt in a house from the day I brought the Israelites up out of Egypt to this day. I have been moving from place to place with a tent as my dwelling. Wherever I have moved with all the Israelites, did I ever say to any of their rulers whom I commanded to shepherd my people Israel, 'Why have you not built me a house of cedar?'" (2 Sam. 7:5–7)

I have to chuckle at this passage because it is like God is saying, "Hey, I am dwelling okay here on my own. I haven't asked you for a temple, so why are you trying to give me one, David?" Oh, how we love to be an all-red room for God sometimes.

There is wisdom in saying no. There is blessing in hearing no too.

Rejection and no are not always bad things. They are often emphasis-making things from the hand of God. I cannot be all things to all people all the time. Neither can you, and neither could King David.

Like King David, my friend Erin has also struggled with this very thing. She had visions of being the perfectly-on-time, Martha Stewart, wearing-stilettos type of mom. So Erin tried to look flawless in her stilettos and live a perfect life while toting two toddlers (who were also going to grow up and be perfect) around town. You can probably guess what she learned along the way. Erin says:

> Rejection and no are not always bad things. They are often emphasis-making things from the hand of God.

64

Eventually, I realized that I had spent so much time "being all things to all people" that I prevented God from molding me into the woman he had designed me to be so many years before. I had ripped that divine paintbrush right out of the ultimate Artist's hands and attempted to paint my own version of life. I can't keep up that "striving" game anymore. I'm not meant to be the world's greatest anything. And I am happy to report to you that I am perfectly fine . . . strike that, I am giddy about that these days. Never have I felt better about lounging in my sweatpants, snuggling with my kiddos, and clinging to the truth that God loves me exactly the way I am.

~Erin Hollis

Erin's giddiness is evident to those who know her. I love watching her enjoy her redesigned life. Be encouraged if you are feeling passed over, unnoticed, or weary from striving. The fact that God gives you and me emphasis makes us significant and proves that God wants to be known and loved by us. God wants us—like Erin—to feel giddy and not just good about our life and about his love for us.

In fact, the passage in 2 Samuel 7 that we looked at earlier revealed that God *willingly* dwelt among the Israelites in a man-made tent. This speaks volumes. God *willingly* wants to be with his couture, one-of-a-kind children. And the less we strive to do *all of the things*, the more we will be able to enjoy time with our God and rest in the unique ways he has designed for us to pop.

> The less we strive to do all of the things, the more we will be able to enjoy time with our God and rest in the unique ways he has designed for us to pop.

God's Promises to David

The scene we looked at from King David's life shows that God will override our plans—even if other people support them—whenever they don't align with his emphasis for us. God will also intervene and say no directly through people's counsel or, yes, through their rejection. This is tough and painful; rejection in any form hurts. But a better or clearer emphasis may come into focus from a season of dismissal too.

God told David he was not to build the temple. First Chronicles 22:8 and 28:3 further reveal this was because David had shed much blood and was a man of war. Despite David's military conquests, David had been God's shepherd and king, thus fulfilling his emphases. God reminded David that he was with him every step of the way and that he would make David's name great (2 Sam. 7:8–13). God also promised David a period of rest and that he would use Solomon, David's son, to build the temple.

God's designs for David's life did not include building a temple. Instead, David's redesigned life was full of pastures, politics, and the penning of psalms that touch countless hearts today. David's emphasis, though it was different from his son Solomon's, was just as beautiful and needed.

How to Pop When Necessary

My emphasis is redesigning homes and hearts with the words of God. What is your emphasis? Are you walking in it? If you've tried to add a pop of color to your corner of the world and God has intervened, why might that be?

Our answers to these questions will vary, but if you are finding yourself continually in a busy season, prone to giving in to all-red-room thinking, or feeling unsure about when or how to use your pop of color, try the following tips:

- *Block the burn.* Just like applying sunscreen to our skin blocks the harmful rays of the sun and prevents our skin from burning, we can block burnout in our heart and prevent ourselves from becoming too red or stressed out by saying no whenever we sense God telling us to do so. If there is any hesitancy in your heart, or if the Holy Spirit is trying to catch your attention with conviction, then ask him to help you say no so you can pop whenever it's time to say yes.

- *Listen and learn.* We may not know when to pop because we aren't asking God and then listening for when he wants us to pop! Pray and ask for opportunities to live out your emphasis. Search the Scriptures and discern what they teach about the varying gifts of the Holy Spirit. Romans 12:6–8; 1 Corinthians 12:8–10, 28; and Ephesians 4:11 are great passages to consider and pray through since they list different types of gifts the Holy Spirit infuses into us. Ask those closest to you if they notice evidence of particular gifts in your life to help you identify them. Seek to learn more about your gifts so you can develop them and use them in God-honoring ways.

- *Wait for the heavy.* The Holy Spirit places heavy burdens or impressions on our hearts. That continual nudge to reach out to a certain person that will not go away? The substantial burden to do a certain something that aligns with a command or exhortation from Scripture? These types of instances are what I call *heavies.*

67

Whenever they happen, consider how best to glorify God via prayer or godly counsel concerning the *heavy* before you. Then obey God in the matter. Doing so is another way you can live out the purposes of your re-designed life.

So if you ever thought that by now you'd be living in *the* city or home of your dreams and making one million dollars and, well . . . you aren't, it's okay to admit your disappointment or feelings of failure to yourself and to your God. Ask him to heal you of those feelings. Realize that you're beautifully gifted to do something else with your life and that God is redesigning you so you can bless the lives of others and bring glory to him.

Don't be all things, just be *you*-things.

Your emphasis matters in God's eyes. May this encourage you whenever your life doesn't go as planned.

Your arms are not here to hold Prada. They're here to hold people. And as you do so, be mindful of the patterns around or within you. Because whenever you see a pattern, you'd better start praying.

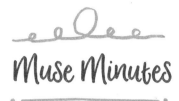

Muse Minutes

1. To help cement principle #2 into that beautiful mind and heart of yours, rewrite in your own words what *emphasis* is here.

   Rewrite in your own words how God uses this principle in our lives.

   List two or three evidences of God's sanctification in your life. Has he disciplined, led, empowered, or changed you in the past? Or are you feeling the pinch of the claw now, and how so?

2. Do you believe that the world is pressuring women to be all things to all people? Why or why not? Have you been told this directly or indirectly? If so, how did this make you feel? What do you think God's message is to women?

3. What is the main emphasis that God has placed on your life right now? Is there anything or anyone hindering you from living out your current emphasis? How can you allow God and then others to help you overcome whatever is hindering you so that you can live out your emphasis?

DESIGN TIP
for Your Home: Color

Ever wonder why some rooms in *Better Homes & Gardens* look cozier than others? Or why some rooms make you feel calmer while others make you feel more productive? It may have something to do with the color of the walls or furnishings used throughout the room. Color is a powerful producer of feelings. So here are some questions to consider when you are trying to figure out what color to paint a room:

- What is the main activity or use of the room? Will you or your guests use the space to work or study in, entertain in, or sleep in?
- What emotion or physical response do you hope to experience while in the space?
- Do you like the overall physical size of the room or do you wish for it to feel smaller or bigger?

How you answer these questions will help guide you as you consider the humongous number of hues available on the market. So, for example, if you want the room to appear larger than it is, use cooler colors (blues, greens, and purples), and keep the contrast within the room to a minimum. If you want to shorten or shrink the size of a room, use warmer colors (reds, oranges, and yellows) throughout, and create contrast throughout the space.[1]

If you want a room that facilitates activity or excitement, add some red to it. If you want to project hospitality and warmth, use yellow or orange somewhere in the room. Or do you want a particular room to help you feel relaxed? Then use green or blue throughout it since these colors are associated with repose, freshness, and calmness.[2]

While I think homes that have mostly white or beige walls are beautiful, I also love homes that have some color on their walls. Pops of color add interest and beauty to a home. Do not be afraid to add some color to your walls, floor, or ceiling trim, or even to your front door. Paint is an easy thing to change, especially if a particular color doesn't end up making you feel as relaxed or productive as you hoped it would.

Pa

ttern

five

Sticking to the Instructions God Gives You

Did you know that working in air traffic control (ATC) is considered one of the most stressful jobs in the world? ATC is ultimately in control of thousands of lives every day. If a controller messes up, planes could crash. Just imagine the pressure controllers are under. No wonder the actors who play them in movies sweat something fierce and smoke a lot of cigarettes. I would be sweating too, but given the fact I ingested used cigarette butts as a wee tot, I have no need to smoke now. Or ever.

A real-life controller, however, sets up a traffic pattern resembling a racetrack in the sky and communicates it to the pilot. Since ATC can see the big picture of where all aircraft in a certain area are located, pilots trust that the pattern given to them is a safe one.

In turn, passengers trust the pilot to follow the route and to land their plane safely. But once ATC gives the pattern, it's up to the pilot whether they will ultimately stick to it, steering to the right or left to land the plane safely. One of the most stressful jobs in the world is based on defined rules and patterns that are set. Imagine what would happen if this was not the case.

I believe one of the other most stressful jobs in the world is just *living*. Amen? Anyone else doing some living through some heartache or disappointment? Mercy. Life *is* hard, and when it doesn't go as planned, we can feel a little sweaty or believe God has abandoned us.

Whenever life shocks or disappoints us, we need direction. Difficult circumstances or emotions like anxiety, grief, or jealousy prevent us from living abundantly, so God may use a repetition of messages from the mouths of others or the pages of Scripture to help us navigate the pain or confusion circling within us.

Thankfully, our God is like a controller who never messes up or takes his eyes off what is happening. Because of his omniscience, God knows everything that has circled, is circling, or will circle around us in this lifetime. Out of his great desire to protect us from something we cannot see or from what can harm us, God relays instructions throughout the pages of the Bible that help us navigate through life's shocks and surprises.

For purposes of this section of the book, I will be using the word *pattern* metaphorically to describe God's commands in verses that repeatedly teach us something about who God is or how we can obey him. Or I will use *pattern* to refer to the behaviors and thoughts that we repeatedly engage in.

With this in mind and like the instructions the ATC relays to a pilot, remember that God's patterns—his commands—

throughout the pages of Scripture are also defined and unchanging. Think what would happen if the opposite were true. There would be no racetrack in the sky for us to follow. We would never know what God is asking of us or if what he has said could change.

Thankfully, even though our patterns of behavior may change or be harmful, God himself is unchanging and his patterns scattered throughout the Bible are permanent. We should follow them, because our actions not only affect us but the lives of others as well. All we need to do is trust what we've been told, turn to the right or the left (Isa. 30:21), and stick to God's pattern whenever life doesn't go as planned.

Pattern: The Repetition of Different Colors, Shapes, Lines, or Images

Patterns can have multiple meanings and elements in design. Repetition focuses on the same object being repeated; patterns are made up from different components which are then repeated in the same way throughout the design.[1]

From paisley scarves around our necks to mosaic tile motifs on the floor beneath our feet, patterns are all around us. This design principle occurs whenever an object, symbol, or color is repeated throughout a room, swatch of fabric, or piece of artwork. Change the pattern, and you change the look of any window treatment, chair, or office cubicle. In fact, patterns are my favorite thing to incorporate into whatever I am designing because they add interest, beauty, and an element of fun into any interior space.

Take, for instance, a children's area in a shopping mall or church nursery. The possibilities of how to make these spaces engage the imagination and spirit of a child are endless. The flooring may consist of carpet tiles that come in a variety of animal prints or in varying shades of blue with air bubbles and fish on them. The repetition of these prints or images help the children's area feel like an underwater or jungle experience.

Patterns are also of great importance to a designer wanting to highlight the uniqueness of the region where a hotel he or she is working on will be located. For example, chair upholstery or a wallpaper border that has repeating diamonds, triangles, or kilim motifs works well for a lobby of a hotel located in the southwestern part of the United States. But if a designer is working on a room or hotel lobby located on the East Coast, they'll use patterns that consist of damask, paisley, toile, or stripes, as the East Coast is more formal or traditional than the Southwest in its style.

God uses patterns of different types in our lives as well. His patterns are meant to catch our attention, teach us, and help us remember who he is and what he desires for our lives. This is by design. God uses repetition in our lives to reengage our mind and our spirit because we sometimes become forgetful and complacent in our faith. Or we rebel by surrounding ourselves with triangles and diamonds when God has asked us to live in the midst of stripes or paisley. Or maybe we think we have everything in order, so God places a person or situation in our path that is full of fluorescent plaid in order to wake us up, prompting us to change.

Although God uses patterns for his purposes, we also sometimes find ourselves in unhealthy patterns of our own creation. For instance, what do we do when we see specific things or thought patterns in our mind happening over and over again? Do we ignore them? Or do we grow from the warnings or messages that God lovingly places before us? I believe that we are to grow from them as my friend Carey has. Doing so enables her to follow patterns of truth as God redesigns her life.

Fighting for Truth

Carey Scott

We all have patterns in our life—those things we do often without knowing it. My family calls them "isms." This could be a certain mannerism, like the way you move your arms or the way you pronounce a word. It could be a favorite route you drive to work without fail or the fact that you order the same type of dish, regardless of the restaurant.

We also have isms in the way we react to situations. My first response is usually defensiveness when someone is critical of me—be it constructive or not. I laugh hysterically when I get scared. And when I watch a movie where an animal is hungry or homeless, I'm a hot mess of tears that cannot be consoled. Sometimes isms can be a bit quirky.

There are patterns we follow with community too, certain people or personality types we tend to gravitate toward. For me, my ism is finding those deep-water girls who are willing to chew on the meaty topics. I hang with women who aren't worried about looking perfect. I love the ones who have a story, often a hard one with lots of heartaches and overcoming. In a group, we'll be the ones sitting in the corner sharing our struggles and challenges with one another. They are my people, and the ones I choose to do life with.

But we can also have isms that threaten to steal our joy and peace. They aren't the cute or quirky kind that make others roll their eyes and giggle at our predictability. Instead, these are the patterns so deeply entrenched they are almost undetectable. Even more, they are dangerous.

At the urging of a friend, I agreed to keep track of any negative thoughts I had about myself for a twenty-four-hour period. She was doing some research to prove that women battle negative thought patterns, and I was her guinea pig. Her theory was simple: women regularly beat themselves up with unspoken words. And because I was sure this wasn't one of my isms, I accepted the challenge. What I discovered shocked me.

The result wasn't just a few negatives here and there. Instead, it was pages full of self-bullying.

In Proverbs 4:23 (GNT), God addresses this: "Be careful how you think; your life is shaped by your thoughts." That list of negative thoughts became a flashlight. It revealed an ism—a pattern—that was casting a shadow on my self-worth. Every time I called myself stupid for losing my keys, or too much for having big feelings, or not enough for letting someone down, my confidence took a hit. And I began to see how I was walking those feelings of self-doubt out every day.

I'm learning to be more aware of patterns in my life. I want to applaud the good ones and stop the negative ones. Life is just too short to self-bully. And because our isms are often routine and habitual, it's important to take inventory of them from time to time.

Even more, we are the glue that holds relationships together. We're the freedom fighters for our friends. We are the ones who train up kids, support husbands, and care for aging parents. We have the opportunity to rule the world with grace and peace. And we can't do that when we're imprisoned by negative patterns.

I'm more aware of my thoughts these days. I'm more careful about the kinds of things I say to myself. And when I begin to see hurtful isms form in my mind, I'm quicker to ask God to replace them with patterns found in Scripture. Doing so helps me learn what God thinks of me and helps me understand who he is. Now I find strength and hope in him whenever something rattles my confidence. I hope the same for you too.

Pattern within the Pages of Scripture

> For this is what the high and exalted One says—
> he who lives forever, whose name is holy:
> "I live in a high and holy place,
> but also with the one who is contrite and lowly in
> spirit,
> to revive the spirit of the lowly
> and to revive the heart of the contrite." (Isa. 57:15)

What beautiful words from the Old Testament book of Isaiah. You might want to memorize and recall them often. God, "the One who is high and lifted up" (ESV), chooses to dwell with us in order to revive us and restore us to himself. This is critical for us to receive and claim, because our circumstances can leave us feeling lonely and abandoned. Many believe that God created the world and then left it and us to our own devices. We may look around our world or even within our own home and feel that God has abandoned us or that he doesn't care. This is not true.

The Bible teaches that God is transcendent, or independent from the universe (Ps. 90:2; Acts 17:24–25). But God is also the immanent or sustaining Creator of it (Col. 1:17). His Spirit dwells within his people and he is present in nature, ensuring that even the lilies and individual blades of grass are "clothed" in what they need to flourish (Ezek. 36:27; Matt. 6:25–30; 2 Tim. 1:14).

One of the greatest evidences that God is present with us and that he cares for us is his repetition of revelation.

General revelation is God's communication of himself to all persons at all times and in all places. Special revelation involves God's particular communications and manifestations of himself to particular persons at particular times, communications and manifestations that are available now only by consultation of certain sacred writings.[2]

Our God is a talker. He is involved in our lives. Romans 1 teaches that in a general sense God reveals himself to us through the natural creation around us. But we also have an ongoing need for more personal and specific communication with God that helps us to understand who he is and what he has planned for us.

Because he longs for us to know him and his plans for us, God speaks to us daily. We may experience an inaudible sense as we listen for his nudge during our prayer time. Or we may understand what he wants us to do in a specific situation via the words of Scripture that we are reading. But God will also intervene in human history, allowing us to see what he had scribbled on his kingdom calendar for a particular day.

For example, it was God who led his people out of Egypt and who parted the Red Sea. He also shut the mouths of lions to ensure the safety of Daniel, his beloved prophet. God called David, a lowly shepherd boy, in from the pasture and made him a mighty king. He sent his one and only Son, Jesus, to this earth, to die on the cross and resurrect from the grave.

Today, God continues to reach and save countless men and women through social media or missionaries with his gospel message. Our God is an efficient and effective communicator. His movement is seen throughout human history and saturates our prayer life and interaction with Scripture. From his repeated revelations we know that God continually provides for, rejoices in, and forgives those who love him.

God's Patterns of Forever, Forgiveness, and Fun

While the specific ways God communicates with us on an individual basis vary, the patterns he designed for us to learn and grow from throughout the pages of Scripture are fixed or unchanging. Thank goodness. My brain is barraged with a myriad of messages from the internet and social media. Add to this my issues of aging and mom brain. I cannot remember all. the. things. Can you?

So my fellow forgetters, here is a sampling of some patterns that left an imprint on my scattered heart. They help me stay strong in my faith, encouraging me whenever I start to wander away from the God I love or whenever life becomes wearisome. A simple Google search will help you discover additional ones on topics like purity, money, prayer, or your identity and purpose in Christ. I decided to touch on the following patterns because they reveal more of who God is.

> As a culture we are becoming increasingly *me* focused instead of *God* focused. No wonder contentment escapes us—we are looking for it in the wrong place.

As a culture we are becoming increasingly *me* focused instead of *God* focused. No wonder contentment escapes us—we are looking for it in the wrong place. Our ultimate purpose or calling in this life is to know and love God. Anything other than him will never completely fulfill us. While some level of contentment can be found within human relationships, lasting contentment is ultimately found in our relationship with God.

We all fail. But God is holy.

We lie or exaggerate. God is honest.

We wound. God heals.

We hold a grudge. God extends grace.

Recognizing and responding to the following patterns puts our focus back on to where it needs to be when life surprises or shocks us—on God and God alone.

God's Pattern of Forever [3]

One of the most beautiful and awesome things about our God is that he *is forever*. He always has been and will always be. There never was a time when he did not exist. There will never be a time when God ceases to be. The great I AM . . . *is*. Time itself and the seasons of this life do not limit or change God. He created them and is separate from them. God never tires or lives under the reality of a learning curve either. How different God is from us!

One of the gravest mistakes we can make is to think God doesn't care or to leave him out of the hot messes we make. But this is sometimes hard for us to avoid. It's been hard for me; there are times when it felt like God was either out to get me or apparently powerless to stop what was happening to me. It's natural to wonder where God is when the proverbial hits of life just keep on coming.

There will be days when we doubt God's availability and ability to be the best, because others do not treat us in the way we think is the best. But to project what others have done to us onto God, assuming he will behave in the same way, is an insult to his goodness, mercy, and holiness. Oh, if only we could begin to grasp the depths of God's love for us. If only we could understand the value he places on every single human life, and the care he's taking to work out his designs in our lives, then we would never point the finger at him when we are mistreated or when relationships in our life fall apart.

Stick to this pattern. Learn it well. Remember and rest in our forever God. Lasting security and peace are found only in him because he is the only everlasting One. I encourage you to give God your offense, anger, or feeling of betrayal the moment it surfaces. Cling to the pattern of *forever* whenever you feel that God doesn't care or when people hurt or disappoint you. It is there to reorient your perspective and to teach you about the permanence of your God. How will you know this pattern when you see it? It will contain words or phrases like the following:

Everlasting

> Before the mountains were born
> or you brought forth the whole world,
>   from everlasting to everlasting you are God. (Ps.
>   90:2)

From the foundation or creation of the world

Father, I want those you have given me to be with me where I am, and to see my glory, the glory you have given me because you loved me before the creation of the world. (John 17:24)

Reign forever and ever

> The LORD reigns
> for ever and ever. (Exod. 15:18)

God's Pattern of Forgiveness [4]

God's forgiveness is another pattern that we need to cling to as life circles about us. There are days when I mess up big-time. I love the New Living Translation of the Bible and how the apostle Paul wrote in Romans 7:14–15, "The trouble is with me, for I am all too human, a slave to sin. . . . For I want to do what is right, but I don't do it. Instead, I do what I hate." For real, Paul. Preach. Sin feels good, maybe even comforting or justifiable in the moment. But it has consequences that are not warm and fuzzy.

To be honest, on most days my sin is all up in my face, making me feel unworthy of God's forgiveness. Some days I shy away from asking God for it when I pray even though forgiveness matters and is important to God. How do I know it is important? Because it has a pattern. God repeatedly mentions the issue of forgiveness throughout Scripture. And because he is a forever God who is always with us, I believe he hates it whenever sin hinders our intimacy with him. Enter God's drive to forgive us of sin. Stick to this pattern. Learn it well. Cease feeling unworthy and consider yourself and others worthy of forgiveness since God extends it to you.

God does not want us to be shy before him, but to be sanctified by him. He desires for us to "pop" for him and to not poop out on him. God never wants us to feel separated from him, but to live securely in him. So whenever you feel burdened under the weight of your sin and unworthy of forgiveness, look for this pattern and for verses in the Bible that contain the words *forgiveness, forgiven,* or *transgressions*: we can learn much from them. An online acquaintance, friend, spouse, or family member may choose not to forgive you, but God will and does. His forgiveness has these characteristics:

It is limitless.

For as high as the heavens are above the earth,
    so great is his love for those who fear him;
as·far as the east is from the west,
    so far has he removed our transgressions from us.
(Ps. 103:11–12)

It is sure and dependable.

If we confess our sins, he is faithful and just and will forgive us our sins and purify us from all unrighteousness. (1 John 1:9)

It stems from the saving and sufficient work of Jesus (not from anything "good" we do or attempt to do).

In him we have redemption through his blood, the forgiveness of sins, in accordance with the riches of God's grace that he lavished on us. With all wisdom and understanding, he made known to us the mystery of his will according to his good pleasure, which he purposed in Christ, to be put into effect when the times reach their fulfillment—to bring unity to all things in heaven and on earth under Christ. (Eph. 1:7–10)

God's Pattern of Fun [5]

Adulting is hard. Thank goodness for laughter. And boy, I sure do love me a good laugh, which usually results from something I did. For example, I sometimes don't speak or apparently understand my native language of English very well. Which is awesome because I am writing in said native language to you.

When I was a little girl I used to watch the nightly news with my dad. Somewhere among the newscasts I misheard an oft-repeated phrase uttered by our meteorologist. For *decades* I would say to others something akin to, "Brrr. It is supposed to be freezing today. I heard that the windshield is going to drop to like -1 degree or something." Did you catch the epic mistake that NO ONE FOR YEARS was kind enough to correct me on? I said "windshield."

A *windshield* is the pane of glass that runs parallel to the front dashboard in your car. I, however, thought *windshield* had two meanings, thanks to the weatherman in Kansas. So I kept saying *windshield* instead of *wind chill* to whoever would listen. I can't even believe I did this. Okay, yes I can.

It was finally my sweet husband who grew me up in weather speak and revealed my linguistic error. I was embarrassed and devastated. And then I laughed at myself for a long time. We still laugh whenever we hear a weatherperson say *wind chill*. Feel free to do the same.

I also pray that you will pause for a minute and consider how much you've allowed yourself to laugh lately. The kind of laughter that makes you snort like a pig or cry tears of joy. When was the last time you relaxed and did something for fun? Not something fun for your bestie, or for your children or spouse, but something that *you* consider to be fun that made you chuckle deeply?

Joy strengthens and sustains. Happiness is fleeting and fickle.

I pray you are making that time to laugh, because our level of laughter is a telling indicator of our level of joy. As our social media feeds have rightly pointed out in a cacophony of memes, happiness and joy are two totally different things. Joy strengthens and sustains. Happiness is fleeting and fickle.

Even though life may not be going according to our plans, God desires for us to be joyful in the midst of the shocks and hurts. Why? Because he is joyful. God is working all things out for our everlasting good and his unending glory. Our God is eternal and forgiving, but he also laughs and is quite funny. This same joyful God is who we, as Christians, claim to love and strive to emulate on a daily basis.

Christians, then, should be the most joyful people on the planet. Not in a way that is overly cheesy, really loud, and in people's faces. But in a more sure-and-steady kind of way. Those who love Jesus know what they have been saved from. They also know that all the things that hurt or frustrate them now will not follow them into eternity. Revelation 21:4 promises no death or tears will exist in heaven. The tears we shed right here and right now are the only ones that we, the children of God, will ever experience. Talk about a joy-producing thought, amen?

Let me be clear, I do not believe God wants us to pretend to be happy in dark seasons of life, faking everyone out while we fall apart inside. However, when we yield to the movement of God, pain and joy can coexist. I will touch on this when we discuss the principle of space in a later chapter, so hang on.

Joy is not surface deep, but soul deep. It doesn't come and go but just is. Joy is not a result of our circumstances, but results in knowing our God and enjoying him no matter our circumstances. It isn't something we can fake or produce within ourselves. It is a God-given gift. Are you asking God to fill the core of your soul with joy? Are you allowing the joy of the Lord to hold you up as you live a life you did not design? And if you are not experiencing some level of joy in your life, why do you think this might be?

Stick to this pattern. Cease trying to be surface-level happy. Ask God to fill you up with his soul-level joy whenever life falls apart, for joy gives us the strength to go on and helps to ease our stress level. And God has filled our world full of things that are fun and people that are just, well . . . funny. Go and enjoy them.

Look for patterns of fun that usually include the words *joy, blessed, delight, pleasure,* or *laughter* throughout the pages of Scripture. They're gratifying to read and teach us several things:

God's joy fulfills us.

I have told you this so that my joy may be in you and that your joy may be complete. (John 15:11)

God rejoices over us.

For the LORD takes delight in his people;
he crowns the humble with victory. (Ps. 149:4)

Laughter is good for our soul.

A cheerful heart is good medicine,
but a crushed spirit dries up the bones. (Prov. 17:22)

Pay attention to and grow from patterns like these. God wants you to know more about him so you can place your confidence in him or experience freedom and joy whenever life doesn't go as planned. Whether you find yourself in a desert season full of diamonds and triangles or in a fancy-schmancy season full of damask and toile, stick to the pattern as God redesigns your life. For this is what God wants us to know, rest in, enjoy, or in some instances obey, so we can navigate whatever is circling around us safely.

six

Replacing Negative Patterns in Your Life

Have you seen the movie *27 Dresses*? This movie is a biographical sketch of my life that I didn't authorize Hollywood to share with you all. The latter part of my single years was spent playing paintball, leading Bible studies, and hanging out by the pool with all my single friends. Besides becoming tan, I was also becoming a professional bridesmaid.

While the number of brightly colored satin dresses in my closet neared the dozen mark, the number of dried bouquets of flowers that I kept catching during wedding reception bouquet tosses also increased. I dated what seemed like every bachelor in the city. And Phoenix is a big place. By the time I turned thirty-one, I resigned myself to the fact that I would be seriously single and in youth ministry for the rest of my days.

Every trip I made down the aisle as a bridesmaid made me wonder if something was indeed wrong with me. A pattern started to occur whenever I found myself at the altar beside another beaming bride. And it wasn't one that matched my smiling and happy exterior. No, my mind was filled with repetitive thoughts that went something like this:

> *You're not pretty enough and just not enough for any man in general. If you were enough you'd be married by now.*
>
> *You're a prude. Sleep with him or you will lose him. No one has to know.*
>
> *You're a ministry leader in the church. You are too independent and intimidating. Submit to a husband? You? Doubtful . . .*
>
> *You're in your thirties; how embarrassing to still be single. Your standards are too high.*
>
> *You need to try harder not to sin so God will bless you with a husband like he is doing for everyone else.*

On and on the pattern played in my mind. Reviewing these same sentiments over and over hurt me emotionally and made my stomach ache. I could no longer see anything of worth in myself. With each failed relationship, my sadness grew. My prayerful petitions for a husband slowed. God was clearly not interested in making me a married woman. All those thought patterns produced within me was shame—shame over who I was and who I clearly wasn't.

Then on one miserable I-am-still-single type of day, a friend phoned to tell me she wanted to set me up with a pilot named Chad Steel. I thought he sounded made up. But we did the long-distance dating thing for several months and I continued to doubt. Me, married? Not going to happen. Ever. And especially to a military man. But Chad loves Jesus and he is "hawt."[1]

Chad's God-given hawtness aside, I watched TV and saw the USAA commercials. Pictures of soldiers coming home from war with their wife standing there waiting and sobbing replayed in my mind. Everyone kept telling me I would be "barefoot and pregnant" and all by myself while my husband would be off in a foreign desert saving the world. I reckoned I could not deal with that. Nope, not going to marry Chad Steel and become a military spouse.

Four months later, Chad proposed to me in front of the Sleeping Beauty Castle at Disneyland. I was so distracted by the fact that Goofy and Donald Duck kept photobombing our pictures and the new, shiny bling on my finger that I forgot to say yes. But I ended up marrying Chad Steel and becoming a military spouse. I became pregnant three months after that and he deployed to a faraway desert to save the world. I waited all those years to get married and then my husband deployed. I laugh about the irony of this now. The day he returned home from overseas I was a crying, very pregnant mess. My life had, in fact, turned into a USAA TV commercial. But we did survive our first year of marriage and I was grateful Chad was there to meet our son minutes after he was born.

I'm now a happily married woman and proud of my husband and of his service to our country. What surprises me though is the fact that negative thought patterns similar to the ones that occurred during my single years still surface in my mind.

Marrying a wonderful man did not erase my shame. Now my negative thought patterns sound more like this:

> *Well, you are not getting any younger, and your body no longer looks like it did on your wedding day. You better work out more and use antiwrinkle cream so your husband will still love you.*
>
> *You are always tired and distracted. Maintain physical intimacy more often with your husband, or you will give him cause to stray if you do not satisfy him.*
>
> *You need to try harder not to sin so God will bless you with a perfect marriage just like he is doing for everyone else.*

Here is what I am learning. Wearing a rock on my left hand has not erased my shame. Calling upon the Rock who created my hands eases it instead.

Seasons of our life change, but the thought patterns that produce negative feelings may not change because we allow them to continue. Negative thought patterns criticize, critique, and crumple the hearts of the single, married, divorced, and widowed alike. Is there a negative thought pattern or behavior in your own life that is coming to mind as you read this right now? Then I pray you will allow God to help you stop it and to let go of it. We must replace a negative pattern with a positive pattern that takes our focus off ourselves and places our focus back on to God.

Oh, and I also have another theory as to why I ended up married to Chad Steel. When I was a little girl, I told my mom I was going to marry my cartoon character crush, Mighty Mouse, because he would fly around and save all the girl mice who were in trouble. Well . . . my husband really does fly around and save people in one sense. See? God did fulfill the desire of my little-girl heart by bringing me a mighty 6'1" man. God really is fun. How I love him for this.

Faith That Catches the Attention of Jesus

I really wish the Gospel accounts in the New Testament were longer. As I reflect on what I do know about Jesus's life, I chuckle as I think about him putting the Pharisees in their place. I'm challenged by many of his parables and by his Sermon on the Mount. And I am often moved by the miraculous ways Jesus healed the lame and the sick. It didn't matter their disability, age, gender, or social status, Jesus healed them. One particular woman on the receiving end of such an encounter has become a personal hero of mine.

The Gospel of Mark tells us that after Jesus healed a demon-possessed man in Gerasenes, he was summoned to the house of Jairus, who was a leader in the synagogue. Jairus's daughter was ill, so he asked Jesus to come and heal her. On the way there, a woman who had been bleeding for twelve years reached out and touched Jesus's garment, and in doing so, she was healed immediately.

As you are about to see, this woman's touch stopped the Son of God in his tracks. The Jewish VIP Jesus was on the way to help had to wait a little longer, because someone who has a whole lot of courage and faith is also a VIP in Jesus's eyes. This woman was no leader in the community, and yet Jesus made time for her. I wish we were told her name or more information about her life before she fell ill. I also wonder if she had any specific thought patterns repeating in her head as a result

of the continuation of her chronic illness. Maybe her thoughts
went something like this:

> *Will I ever be well again? What did I do to deserve this?
> Why me?*
>
> *My money is gone; how will I survive?*
>
> *Why have I suffered so much under the care of countless
> doctors? Why can't they help me?*
>
> *Could what I am hearing about Jesus of Nazareth be true?
> Can Jesus heal me? If he does heal me, my life will be
> so different!*

What we do know is that this woman suffered from a chronic
illness that caused her to bleed for twelve years. She fell into
a pattern of seeing doctor after doctor, believing they would
be able to help her, but none of their care worked. In fact, the
woman grew worse and, by the time we meet her in Scripture,
had spent all of her money in repeated efforts to be cured. But
then the woman heard about Jesus. In the end, she was healed.
And her faith stopped Jesus in his tracks.

> When she heard about Jesus, she came up behind him in the
> crowd and touched his cloak, because she thought, "If I just
> touch his clothes, I will be healed." Immediately her bleeding
> stopped and she felt in her body that she was freed from her
> suffering.
>
> At once Jesus realized that power had gone out from him.
> He turned around in the crowd and asked, "Who touched my
> clothes?" . . .
>
> Then the woman, knowing what had happened to her, came
> and fell at his feet and, trembling with fear, told him the whole

truth. He said to her, "Daughter, your faith has healed you. Go in peace and be freed from your suffering." (Mark 5:27–30, 33–34)

While we may not know the exact pattern of thoughts that replayed in this woman's mind, we do know she was desperate to be healed. Maybe her negative or shameful thought patterns started to slow and were replaced with hopeful and more positive ones that focused on Jesus. Which, in turn, motivated her to go and see him.

And so here we find her risking ridicule and placing herself smack-dab in the middle of the crowd because this is where Jesus was, and because she was desperate to meet him. I love that it was Jesus who wound up looking for her since her faith touched him in ways we cannot understand or comprehend. I wish Scripture told us how this woman lived out the rest of her redesigned life. I bet you she wasn't excluded anymore, but included instead. She was no longer unclean but healed. Kind of like the other unnamed woman who came to the dinner party and washed the feet of Jesus with her tears, the one we looked at in chapter 2. Hmm . . . I see a pattern here, don't you?

In the same way, Jesus, along with God the Father and the Holy Spirit, notices every single touch of desperation we extend his way. It doesn't matter how much the Holy Trinity has on their proverbial plate, or if someone who the world deems to be a VIP

> It doesn't matter how much the Holy Trinity has on their proverbial plate, or if someone who the world deems to be a VIP needs their help at the same time we do. God makes time for you.

needs their help at the same time we do. God makes time for you. Jesus knows your desperation. The Holy Spirit can ease your conscience or heal your body, whether or not you ask for him to do so. But in this particular passage, Jairus had to ask Jesus to come. The woman had to risk and touch Jesus.

Are you desperate for God? Will you ask or risk in order to be close to your Healer? Or are you looking to your own version of a cartoon Mighty Mouse instead of your Mighty Savior to rescue you while nursing a negative thought or behavioral pattern? This is vital for you to realize, because this is a fact: life will not go as we planned for it to go.

Seasons full of pain and disappointment are prime times for negative patterns to take root and grow. So watch for them.

I also know that some of you are like this woman and suffer from a chronic illness. There are precious ones close to me who do, and it breaks my heart to hear of their ongoing pain. I don't know why doctors are unable to help them or why their suffering continues. I wish they could reach out and literally touch the robe of Jesus like this woman from Scripture was able to do. But I know that their Mighty Savior is moved by their faith and is using their story to touch the lives of those of us who are privileged enough to know them. Their faith and ability to endure and achieve much in their lives is beautiful and inspiring. They are courageous warriors in their own beautiful, couture way and are deserving of our prayers and respect.

But for others of us, we have not asked Jesus to come and heal us. It could be that our suffering has gone on for way too long because we are stuck in a pattern of thinking or behaving that does not align with the directions our heavenly ATC has given us. We are just circling aimlessly, unable to land at the destination God desires for us. Whenever we see a pattern, we better pray and pay attention to whether it is true and helpful or false and hurtful.

Patterns Are Powerful

We are created to bless the world around us in a myriad of ways. Negative patterns prevent us from doing so. So we shouldn't ignore or blow past them, but pray through and release them into the capable, healing hands of God.

I don't pretend to know what you may be dealing with. I believe some of us need to seek professional and medical help to enable us to heal and break free from certain negative patterns. God heals through medicine and uses professional services all the time. And should you, as a Christian, choose to use these wonderful resources, it doesn't mean you have less faith than your pastor or that you are a failure in the eyes of God. But also consider studying and knowing the patterns of the Bible to help you heal and overcome as well. God has taken the time to communicate them to you and me for a reason.

The more you study God's Word, the more patterns you will find to help you overcome the negative ones in your life. For example, to replace a pattern of dishonesty with a pattern of honesty, check out verses such as Exodus 20:16; Proverbs 12:22; and Colossians 3:9. To replace a pattern of impatience with a pattern of patience, check out verses such as Romans 12:12; Colossians 3:12; and Ephesians 4:2. Or to replace a pattern of anger with a pattern of love, check out verses such as Proverbs 3:3–4; 1 Corinthians 13:4–5; and 1 Peter 4:8. I encourage you to keep a journal full of the patterns you find in Scripture so that you can refer to them often when life surprises or shocks you. They are there, if we only slow ourselves down enough to see them.

I love how my friend Gretchen is slowing herself down and releasing control to God. By doing so, Gretchen has discovered the peace of God and is resting in new patterns of faithfulness, perseverance, and gratitude. She says:

> When life was seemingly under my control, I felt at peace. Consequently, as life grew wild and chaotic as the sea, this became my undoing. I had spent most of my adult life trying to control the patterns of those around me in order to enjoy a peaceful existence. In the midst of a life I may not have designed, I learned that peace is not found in controlling the patterns of others but rather through allowing God to redesign the patterns in me. He taught me how to respond wisely when my security felt threatened. *Faithfulness*, *perseverance*, and *gratitude* became my default pattern. This allowed me to experience contentment no matter how unpredictable life became. I may not be able to design the picture-perfect life of my choosing but I can still find the peace that surpasses all understanding. Come to find out, that's even better.
>
> ~Gretchen Fleming

I agree with Gretchen: God's peace *is* better. And when life doesn't go as planned, we are in need of it the most. I trust you agree and that you'll take a moment to pause and ask God to fill you with his peace that really does surpass our understanding.

How to Check for and Replace Negative Patterns in Your Life

How can we know if we are circling about in a negative pattern? Begin with these suggestions:

- *Notice how the pattern makes you feel.* Does a thought make you feel shameful, discouraged, ugly, vengeful, envious or jealous, selfish, prideful, unlovable, or unforgiveable? Then it needs to go! God desires for us to be loving, humble, patient, forgiving, supportive of, and gentle toward others and toward ourselves.

- *Seek the counsel of others.* What do others think or what would they think about the pattern in question if you told them about it? I encourage you to reach out to safe and trusted godly friends, a mentor, a counselor, or a pastor and ask their opinion whenever you can't shake a certain thought or behavior. Getting a fresh, outside perspective is helpful because someone else may see your reality differently than you do. Perhaps they've struggled in the same way, or maybe they can point you to a positive pattern that you can dwell on, quickening your ability to get rid of whatever is negative.

- *Consider what Scripture says.* Whenever you see a pattern, pray for discernment and ask the Holy Spirit for strength to cease nursing the negative. Then use verses like Philippians 4:8 to filter your thoughts:

Finally, brothers and sisters, whatever is true, whatever is noble, whatever is right, whatever is pure, whatever is lovely, whatever is admirable—if anything is excellent or praiseworthy—think about such things.

If the belief is *not* true, it goes. Let it go and move your thoughts on to something else. The same applies if your thinking isn't pure or lovely or any of the other things mentioned in this verse. When I am in a season where I am really struggling with my thoughts, I write this verse on a note card and keep the card with me. Then when the unhealthy pattern starts happening, I start filtering the negative thought through this verse. Over time, the pattern and perspective regarding myself, the situation, or the other person changes and I am quicker to think whatever is positive, true, or right regarding myself or the situation.

Stick to the Pattern

I hope the design principle of pattern reinforces the truth that God is not a distant and uncaring God. He most certainly cares and is present, desiring to communicate with you and me so we can know more about who he is and about how we can live a life of peace, freedom, and blessing. No matter what state your human affairs are in, you have a God who is everlasting, forgiving, and who rejoices over you. He sees you and loves you.

Consider if there's a pattern about God that you need to hang in a prominent place in your heart. I also pray you will take some time to see if there are patterns that are circling within you. Will you allow God to speak to you through them? Once you hear him, all you have to do is turn to the right or to the left and stick to the pattern.

Once you hear him, all you have to do is turn to the right or to the left and stick to the pattern.

And don't be surprised if you brush up against someone who is hard to love or who is opposite of you while circling in the pattern. Sometimes we think we're seeing things clearly, when in fact, we're not. Hence our need for the next principle of contrast—and for some new spiritual glasses.

Muse Minutes

1. To help cement principle #3 into that beautiful mind and heart of yours, rewrite in your own words what *pattern* is here.

   Rewrite in your own words how God uses this principle in our lives.

2. If you are in a painful season, filter it through the following patterns and record how they can specifically help you persevere through whatever is happening. Or if life is dandy, how can these patterns help you persevere in future seasons that will be hard?

Pattern of forever:

Pattern of forgiveness:

Pattern of fun:

Also consider this: What would it mean if these patterns of God were not true? What if God wasn't for "forever"? What if he did not forgive? And heavens, what if God was not fun? I shudder to think what this would mean.

3. Here's an additional pattern I encourage you to look up and learn: the pattern of God's fortification or protection. God is our ultimate defender, rock, fortress, or protector. Scripture will use varying words within this pattern, but what a comfort it is to know that God has our back. I encourage you to remember that God is on your side whenever you feel outnumbered or think that all is lost. Look up the following verses and see if you can find additional ones within the pattern of fortification: Psalm 34:19; 46:1; 91:2; Isaiah 54:17; and 2 Thessalonians 3:3.

DESIGN TIP
for Your Home: Texture

Women often want their home to feel feminine, but they may not want to decorate with floral patterns and lace. Or you may have a man living with you who does not appreciate having doilies and pink everywhere! Bless him. Deep breaths. You can still have feminine without the fluff. You can still have masculine without animal heads and sports memorabilia on every wall too. Here is where texture comes into play.

All objects have a visual or perceived texture to them that allows your eyes to *feel* the space before your hands do. To add a casual vibe that will make your man feel more at ease, consider textures that are rough, sturdy, or rugged. Think of adding wood, stucco, or stone on the floor, walls, or horizontal counter space. For a more traditional or feminine feel without the frills use fine, smooth, or soft textures or curved shapes throughout the space. Can you mix textures? Absolutely. In fact, most contemporary spaces have a mix of both.[2]

Co

ntrast

seven

Seeing God More Clearly

I can remember the first time I put my glasses on. The images around me became clearer and crisper. I could finally read the words splattered across giant billboards along the highway. Individual leaves on trees came into focus again. The world around me was no longer blurry. Prior to wearing glasses, I falsely believed I was seeing the world around me clearly, but I wasn't. The contrast between what I could see without my glasses versus what I could see with them on was huge.

In the same way, the focus of our heart and mind becomes blurred whenever we allow things like unrealistic expectations or pride to affect how we view God, our life, or other people. Our God longs to help us see him and all that happens in our lives clearly. Because of that, God allows contrast to happen within and around us as part of our sanctification and uses it to ultimately turn our focus back to him. The longer we follow, love, and obey God, the clearer we'll be able to see. This is by design.

Things within and around us should start to look different as we view them through the lens of God's personhood and perspective. His ways are often different from our ways of doing things. Not only is there contrast within and around us, there's also contrast within the personhood of God himself. We'd be wise to embrace all the complexities of our God, for doing so increases our awe, trust, and security in him.

The focus of our heart and mind becomes blurred whenever we allow things like unrealistic expectations or pride to affect how we view God, our life, or other people.

As with the other principles in this book, we should welcome contrast whenever we see its presence in our life. We may think we are perceiving things clearly. But maybe we're not. Thankfully, our gracious God notices when we're unable to see our reality correctly. He has designed contrast into our lives by allowing things like unmet expectations and/or dissatisfaction with things that once fulfilled us, or by bringing people who are wired differently than we are into our lives. Though what it reveals may sting, this principle helps us to see ourselves, our God, and those around us in a much clearer, truer sense when life doesn't go as planned.

Contrast: Opposites That Catch Our Attention

Contrast in art refers to the positioning of opposing components in a work of art. It occurs when two or more related elements are strikingly different. The greater the difference the greater the contrast.[1]

Similar to patterns, physical examples of contrast are easy to spot and are quite prevalent in artwork or in the interior spaces around us. When used correctly, this principle creates variety, drama, and interest within a room or piece of artwork. It helps to make an element more intense or noticeable. A designer or artist will use objects of opposite sizes, textures, shapes, or colors to achieve contrast.

Take, for instance, what happens when complementary colors are used together. Imagine the "color wheel" that you probably learned about in your high school art class. Complementary colors are across from each other on the wheel. The complement of red is green. Yellow's complement is purple, and the complement of orange is blue.

Let's say you go to the store to buy some new pillows for your living room couch. You see one pillow that has orange and blue stripes on it. The pillow beside it is orange-and-white striped. On which pillow does the orange appear brighter or bolder? Which pillow is more dramatic? The orange-and-blue one, of course! The color orange appears more dramatic or intense because it contrasts more with the color blue than it does with the color white.

Or, imagine thirteen-by-thirteen-inch floor-tile patterns done in the contrasting colors of black and white. I recently visited an office building that had black-and-white-checkered marble flooring in all of its hallways. It was stunning and dramatic, unlike most office buildings, which typically use the same color of carpet throughout their hallways.

Most corporate hallways are monotonous for sure, but too

much contrast can also be a bad thing—it can make a room feel disjointed or overwhelming. And a space that lacks contrast acts like camouflage, making everything blend in a little too much. In other words, no contrast = a boring room or piece of art.

Likewise, we see contrast between who we were before knowing Christ and who we are as forgiven children of God. Regardless of how checkered our pasts are, 2 Corinthians 5:17 says, "Therefore, if anyone is in Christ, the new creation has come: The old has gone, the new is here!" I love this. The old us is gone. The new us, being sanctified into the likeness of Jesus Christ, is our present and future reality. The level of contrast between what we used to be and who we are now should become more evident as the years pass. In addition, God will bring people and circumstances into our lives that are the opposite of us, or opposite of what we wanted or hoped for, to help us mature in godliness and to help us see him and ourselves a little clearer.

I believe the hard-to-love person, a broken dream, or unmet expectations may be the divine set of glasses that God is asking us to look through for a while. They may be the very thing we need to help us see better—and, in turn, help others around us see better too.

Fellow spectacle wearer, we are in the world, but not forever dwellers of it. We were once blinded by the things that matter to the world but clearly see now the things that matter in heaven. We grieve but do so with hope. We have the power to turn the other cheek instead of retaliating and fighting back. And we have the ability to overcome sin while choosing not to indulge in it. This is what contrast produces within us. I dig it and want it for the both of us big-time. Why?

You and I are designed to stand out. A child of God does not belong in camouflage. No, give us some orange and blue or

> *You and I are designed to stand out. A child of God does not belong in camouflage.*

red and green to wear. People should see the difference in us the longer we live out God's designs for us, causing them to wonder why we believe and live the way that we do.

We are not to fit in with the rest of the world, nor are we supposed to be "normal," whatever that means. There is nothing boring or predictable about us, our God, or our redesigned life. We were created to be couture, or one of God's kind.

Lord, help us to really see.

We *are* contrast.

Parenting the Child I've Been Given

Teri Lynne Underwood

"Parent the child you have, not the child you wanted," she told me as I sat next to her, my belly bulging with the miracle baby we'd been told we would never have. I remember thinking that the child I was having was the one I wanted, the one I'd longed to have for almost five years.

When I nursed Casiday as an infant, I told her about all the adventures we'd have, all the ways I'd encourage and support her, all the dreams and plans I had for her. I sang all the old hymns over her, hoping to embed in her heart from day one the truths of God's amazing grace and how great is his faithfulness.

But as she got older, something happened I hadn't included in my plans. Casiday Hope became her own little person with her own personality, preferences, and plans. And sometimes, her dreams for her life didn't match what I'd so carefully spoken over her during those late-night feedings.

In many ways, she was almost the opposite of what I'd imagined my child would be. And I had to make a decision: Would I parent the child I have or the one I'd always thought I wanted? I wish I could say I'd quickly and definitively chosen the former. But the truth is, letting go of all those expectations and plans didn't always come easily.

I wasn't always the mom I hoped I would be. I've said and done things I would give anything to erase. There have been days when I forgot to give grace and days when I held on to my expectations far longer than I should have.

But there is this beautiful truth, even in all the messiness of imperfect mothering: the child I have (and the mom she has) are just what God designed. He knew Casiday was who I needed to remind me to slow down and savor the moments instead of rushing through life. And he also knew she'd need me to push her to try the scary things and to hold on to his Word when life is overwhelming.

In just a few weeks, she'll graduate from high school and I'll move into parenting an adult child. (All those people who said, "Don't blink!" were right.) I've thought a lot lately about the wise friend who reminded me to parent the child I'd been given. Because whatever I imagined about the mom I'd be and the child I'd have, not one of those dreams can begin to compare to the eighteen years of unimaginable joy and inexplicable beauty I've had watching this girl of mine move into adulthood.

Contrast within the Pages of Scripture

I love how Teri Lynne has embraced the fact that her parenting journey is turning out different *and better* than she originally planned. Teri Lynne also grew in her appreciation of God's providence—that when he gives a gift that is exactly opposite of what we want to unwrap, it has a potential and a beauty all of its own.

Let's unwrap a little more about God's personhood because it too contains a good type of contrast. For example, God is not *just* love, or *only* love. Our God is also wise, merciful, and patient. All of these attributes of God gel well together. But then I started to wonder if there's another dimension of his personhood that contrasts with some of these attributes. So far we've seen how each of the design principles mentioned in the book is found in the ways or personhood of God. Can this principle be found in him too? Yes! Our God is also a God of wrath, which stands in contrast to him being a God of love.

The Contrast of God: His Love

Dear friends, let us love one another, for love comes from God. Everyone who loves has been born of God and knows God. Whoever does not love does not know God, because God is love. (1 John 4:7–8)

I was glued to my television screen hours before I sat down to write this section of the chapter. Prince Harry of England married the beautiful Meghan Markle in front of a worldwide audience. The ceremony was beautiful. Commentators were quick to offer their critiques of the day, saying the wedding ceremony had Meghan's influence all over it. It was not the typical English wedding due to many reasons, one of which included the fiery sermon given by American Bishop Michael Curry. He passionately and clearly proclaimed the love of God to every single one of us. I had tears. In a world that continually tries to silence the gospel, there it was, uttered in the midst of the British monarchy and on live TV for an audience of 3 billion. Our God is truly unstoppable. And as the good reverend pointed out, our God is love.

I'd venture to say that most of those watching the wedding were nodding and agreeing. Love, itself, is not a foreign concept to us, for we all experience it. Theologically speaking, the love of God means that he is a giver. Why and what does God give? He gives us more of himself "in order to bring about blessings or good for others."[2]

In fact, I bet that you're probably living in a house or apartment and that you have clothes to wear and food to eat. Given the material blessings in your life, you would generally say that yes, God loves you and cares for you. However, the Bible teaches that the ultimate example of God's love for us is not evidenced by things like finding a good parking spot at Target or in having a home or satisfying job.

No, the ultimate and radical proof of his love involved him sacrificing his beloved Son, Jesus, on a cross. Whether a sermon is being presented at a royal wedding or in a regular Sunday church service, any message about the love of God will be well received. But how well received would the sermon be if it focused on the wrath of God? Wrath? Our God of love is a God of wrath? Why, yes, yes he is. Many are offended or dismiss this attribute of God. But I don't want us to miss this because it matters.

The Contrast of God: His Wrath

The wrath of God is being revealed from heaven against all the godlessness and wickedness of people, who suppress the truth by their wickedness. (Rom. 1:18)

The love of God deserves our attention, worship, and gratefulness for sure. But there is a good and different type of contrast within the personhood of God. Just like the contrast between the pre-Christian "us" and the redeemed "us" is essential, there is contrast within the personhood of God himself that is also crucial.

Yet if God loves all that is right and good, and all that conforms to his moral character, then it should not be surprising that he would hate everything that is opposed to his moral character. God's wrath directed against sin is therefore closely related to God's holiness and justice. God's wrath may be defined as follows: *God's wrath means that he intensely hates all sin.*[3]

The wrath of God isn't exactly something we talk a lot about at Bible study or on our social media feeds. But if we say we love God, then we love *all* of who God is. This includes his wrath, which I realize is unsettling to think about. My friend and Bible teacher, Katie, agrees. As we talked this out, we came up with the following analogy that helps put the wrath of God into perspective.

Imagine that we are best friends with Prince Harry and his wife, Meghan. For a wedding gift we got them a brand-new white couch for one of their many living rooms. Well, I am assuming they have many, many living rooms. This is just a hunch, though. Now imagine Harry's niece and nephews run into the living room with chocolate-covered hands that they proceed to place all over the new white couch. Oh my goodness, there is no way to hide the handprints. They are offensive and may have stained the couch for good.

Now reimagine the same scene, but this time we gifted Harry and Meghan with a brown leather couch instead. Same thing happens. Only this time the handprints aren't as offensive because they blend in. So we may not notice them or be slower to clean them up because they blend in better.

Our world is like the brown leather couch. Our God is like the white couch. We can't change the fact the handprints on the white couch are offensive. We cannot change our God either.

Our culture and the world seem to be lessening the seriousness and offensiveness of sin. We don't want to talk about it or notice it. So we water it down. Meanwhile, its stains are all over the place and people's lives continue to be ruined because of it. Sin and acts of evil are in direct opposition to everything that God is. Therefore, God despises acts of evil and will ultimately judge unrighteousness, because his holiness stands in stark contrast to sin. God cannot tolerate it because he knows sin ruins us, whom he loves.

> Our culture and the world seem to be lessening the seriousness and offensiveness of sin. We don't want to talk about it or notice it.

Similarly, whenever we feel hatred toward the sin or injustices in our world ourselves, we are imitating God's wrath (to a lesser degree, of course), since he feels the same toward these things. I remember watching the news about the Columbine High School shooting and about the Sandy Hook Elementary School shooting that took the lives of twenty precious children. I was filled with anger toward the shooters for taking the lives of those students. I'm sure you feel the same when news like this hits.

It's our hatred or disgust of evil, then, that often motivates us to speak out or act out against the injustices in this world. To feel indifferent toward evil would cause us to do nothing. So we act, and God does the same. God not only disciplines or punishes evildoers himself, he uses entities like our judicial system, military, and law enforcement to help regulate injustices and to carry out some of these consequences as well.

God's wrath is in reaction to sin and evil. It is reserved for the wicked and ungodly who reject him (Exod. 32:9–10; Rom. 1:18; Col. 3:5–6). It is not part of who he is because he is hormonal, has bad days, or is unloving.

The Bible teaches that Jesus bore the wrath of God for us upon the cross. God's wrath is not, nor will it ever be, directed at those of us who love him and who have surrendered their lives in faith to Jesus Christ (Rom. 8:1).

Our God is patient, ultimately wishing that everyone would turn to him, repent, and receive his forgiveness for their sin (2 Pet. 3:9). Why? Because God is also loving, merciful, and gracious. Our God is perfectly complex, isn't he? He is not more of one attribute over another. And so naturally, there is contrast in him that is complementary and purposeful.

Too many people imagine a Hallmark version of God and don't understand his wrath. As a result, they don't take their sin or the gospel message seriously. Some tragically die without knowing the truth and obtaining saving faith in Christ, placing them under the wrath of God. This is why you and I must tell people about both the love and wrath of God. His contrasts are essential from an eternal perspective.

Our Own Road to Damascus, and Why It Matters

One of my favorite stories in the New Testament focuses on what happened to Saul, who became the apostle Paul, as he was traveling to Damascus. It was on the road to Damascus that the Lord literally blinded him and asked Saul why he saw fit to persecute him. See, Saul thought himself righteous while followers of Jesus were blasphemous. God allowed him to carry on like this for a while. Then God moved, or, well . . . confronted and blinded Saul. Why? Because God had a different kind of part or emphasis that Saul needed to play.

Paul went from being a persecutor of Christians to becoming a staunch proponent of Christianity, helping to spread the gospel message of Jesus Christ throughout the Roman Empire. Paul was given a second chance and encountered the love of Christ. He immediately lived a redesigned life. What happened to Paul on the road to Damascus wasn't part of Paul's plan. But it was always part of God's design for Paul's life.

Paul humbled himself before God and spent the rest of his life loving on the same people he used to persecute. The contrast between who Paul used to be and who he ended up being astounds me. Not only did Paul go on to build and strengthen the early church, he also penned many of the books of the New Testament, which continue to instruct and encourage our hearts today. Paul later admitted the following about himself in 1 Timothy 1:15–16:

> Here is a trustworthy saying that deserves full acceptance: Christ Jesus came into the world to save sinners—of whom I am the worst. But for that very reason I was shown mercy so that in me, the worst of sinners, Christ Jesus might display his immense patience as an example for those who would believe in him and receive eternal life.

Paul saw the contrast within himself, embraced it, and grew from it. In doing so, he found contentment and the courage to live out his emphasis. I wonder, can you relate to Paul and to the words he wrote about himself? Have you had a moment where you met God face-to-face on your own type of Damascus road? Were you once a skeptic of God and now consider yourself to be his child?

I know this section of the book is a toughie. There is no condemnation in Christ Jesus (Rom. 8:1), so to bring some on you is not the point of this chapter. But the Bible explains that we are to teach and to speak truth to one another, pray for one another, and hold each other accountable for how we are living our faith out (Prov. 27:17; Eph. 4:15–16, 25; James 5:16). I do not want you to just *feel* good, I want you to *become* God's good, inimitable version of yourself. I want us to mature in our faith and become holier and more glorifying to God. I don't want you to be blind to what is going on in your heart or mind or in your relationships.

> We will not be able to experience contentment, peace, or blessing if there's sin in our life that's robbing us of seeing letters on billboards and leaves on trees.

My prayer for this chapter and the next is that they would help you to see yourself as you truly are. Not for the purposes of self-condemnation but for purposes of self-evaluation. I know my capacity to sin is great, making my need for the Holy Spirit continuous. But I also know that God is patient toward me as I work through my sin and that his grace and love for me are unending. The same is true for you. We're full of some contrast, aren't we? Again, this is by design. We will not be able to experience contentment, peace, or blessing if there's sin in our life that's robbing us of seeing letters on billboards and leaves on trees.

So I encourage you to pause before you read the next chapter. Take an honest look at the condition of your heart. This may be a much-needed "road to Damascus" moment for you. Spend some concentrated time in prayer and ask God to restore your vision. Is there sin such as envy, jealousy, pride, gossip, impurity, or impatience in your life? Could it be unmet expectations and the resulting offense because God or someone you love didn't do what you wanted them to do? What is clouding your vision?

Things will only remain the same if we remain the same.

Blah.

Blurred.

You shouldn't be the same person you were months or even a year ago. So let's do some heart work even if you think you are doing pretty good, or that your sin isn't as bad as someone else's. Sin is sin. It will leave its chocolaty smudges all over our hearts or all over other people. And sin will interrupt, detour, or delay the plans God has designed for us. His purpose for contrast, then, is to prompt us to repent so we can get back to popping for him. May God help us to understand ourselves so that whenever life doesn't go as planned we can see clearly and allow the Holy Spirit to help us correct whatever is blurry within us.

eight

Embracing Your Reality

I am not a gifted cook. Nor am I a cook in any sense of the word. The only time I feel abandoned by God is when I am in the kitchen trying to decipher a recipe and prepare a meal for my family. As I write out our weekly grocery list I flip through my recipes and peruse the ingredients first, since I have usually heard of things like *bread* and *butter* and that leaves me feeling pretty confident. But then the directions ask me to do things like *barding* or *blanching* or to whip up a *bouquet garni*.

What?

Confidence gone.

These words are mean and weird just like the words *mayonnaise* and *moist*. Gag. But cooking is not the only thing that shakes my confidence. Motherhood does too.

For most of my life my thoughts and plans centered on ballet, or on my studies, or on owning a design firm in New York City. Certain friends of mine, however, were eager to marry, start families, and stay at home with their babies. So while I was wearing a plethora of bridesmaid dresses and playing paintball with hormonal teens, some of my friends were studying brands of diapers and cutting out Babies "R" Us coupons. I would smile and nod as they talked about baby names and nursery themes so I would appear just as excited about motherhood as they were. But in reality, I wasn't sure if motherhood was for me.

Babysitting or working in the church nursery was never my thing. And remember that I planned on having a ten-foot waterfall wall with a reflecting pool in the middle of my living room. I honestly saw myself gliding through the next couple of years in tight-fitting skinny jeans instead of stretchy pregnancy pants. I felt guilty for this. Was I missing a mom gene or something? I assumed all of this meant that God was not going to allow me into the motherhood club.

So when I started becoming extremely nauseous four months after I married Chad, I honestly thought my cooking was to blame. But no, I was pregnant with my son. Twenty-three months after he was born, my daughter was delivered safely into my arms. I included the word *safely* in that last sentence for a reason. Both of my pregnancies had their share of complications. My doctor felt that future pregnancies would not be the wisest or safest way to grow our family. This was hard to hear at first, but I knew in my gut that the doctor was right. As I write these words, I remain a doting mama of two and am incredibly grateful that God handpicked me to raise my Jackson and Katie.

Once again, life was turning out differently than I had expected. I was no longer a perfectly groomed, on-time, professional woman. Instead, I found myself in a new season fraught with weird-sounding words like *Bumbo*, *Boppy*, and *Butt Paste*. Again, what? Confusion ensued on many occasions. I eventually figured out what all those weird things were via my new gang of MOPS peeps and I came to appreciate and apply Butt Paste onto my kiddos like a boss.

I also remember my babies' first smiles and their first word, which happened to be *dada*. I remember when they both discovered their shadow for the first time. Their first coos and first steps left me in awe. The pucker faces that quickly appeared as they tasted carrot puree for the first time left me in stitches. Those early years left me sleep and shower deprived, but I was discovering that motherhood was indeed a blessing and most definitely for me.

Over the years my family has endured dozens of mom and Pinterest fails manufactured by yours truly. For example, on one glorious we-were-totally-running-behind kind of day, I ended up inserting two contacts into the same eye. This, of course, made us late to MOPS because I couldn't see that well and could not figure out why. On another mommy-is-losing-it kind of day I forgot to put my son in his crib for his nap, because his baby sister needed my attention. I opened the door to his room hours later only to find the lights still on and him fast asleep, and on the floor directly beside his crib curled up in a ball. His little arm was extending up into the air and was wedged between the slats of his crib. Why? Because he was holding on to the edge of his favorite blanket, which was still in the crib where he too should have been. It was pathetic. I think I heard melancholy violin music playing as I stared at the scene before me . . .

I've also let both of my babies roll off the couch even though I was right beside them. And I watched my toddler "ride" his airplane scooter down our long and steep set of stairs. Watching him topple was like one of those slow-motion scenes from *The Matrix*. I froze. It was not pretty. Why wasn't I watching him more closely? I felt like such a loser mom.

When I first found out I was pregnant, I desired to be a perfect mom too. But motherhood, more than anything else, has taught me that I am nowhere near perfect. There are days when I ask my children to do something with my Mary Poppins voice, only to end up speaking in a loud, foreboding Darth Vader voice because they refuse to obey. Remember the painting I talked about in chapter 1? The one of the screaming figure? I do not mean to make light of yelling here, but I sure do look like him on days when the struggle between my kids and me is real.

And there was also another season of motherhood I didn't see coming. A couple years ago, I had to admit to myself that I did not know how to help one of my children thrive. I believe that a mother usually knows what is best for her child. However, one of my children woke up with a developmental problem that literally appeared overnight and I panicked. I honestly had no idea what to do or how to help my child. I no longer knew what was best.

Over the years our precious one has been tested for various things but nothing conclusive has been discovered. Enlisting the assistance of various therapists has helped some, and I am so grateful for how they have loved my child. I do thank God for these people and continue to trust that God has great things in store for both of my children's lives. Even so, to hear the words *special needs* was heartbreaking. I immediately wondered if what was happening was caused by something I'd done while pregnant.

On top of the guilt was fear. Would my child have a normal life? And then came the anger and all the whys. Why, God? Why my child? This isn't what I had planned. I do not talk or write about this portion of my motherhood journey often. It's still too tender, but we're making it. I refuse to stop helping or believing in my child who is made in the image of a God who faithfully gives *all* children, "special needs" or not, the same hope and future that he gives to the rest of us.

There is definitely a contrast between what I thought motherhood and being a mom was going to be like and how motherhood has actually been. I'm learning that while being on time, looking presentable, and having a clean home and well-behaved children are delightful things, what is the condition of my heart like?

Let's take a peek at two other mothers mentioned in the pages of Scripture. The states of their hearts and how they acted out their love for their sons stand in stark contrast to each other.

The Reality of Our Desire to Control and Manipulate

Now Rebekah was listening as Isaac spoke to his son Esau. When Esau left for the open country to hunt game and bring it back, Rebekah said to her son Jacob, "Look, I overheard your father say to your brother Esau, 'Bring me some game and prepare me some tasty food to eat, so that I may give you my blessing in the presence of the LORD before I die.' Now, my son, listen carefully and do what I tell you: Go out to the flock and bring me two choice young goats, so I can prepare some tasty food for your father, just the way he likes it. Then take it to your father to eat, so that he may give you his blessing before he dies." (Gen. 27:5–10)

Rebekah, Rebekah. Oh mama. You are a cunning one. Deceiving your own husband and prone to favoritism. You had quite the pair of boys to raise. But are you that different from us? Not entirely. Like Rebekah, we sometimes favor one person over another person. Our personality or politics do not gel well with someone else's, so we do not expend the same amount of energy on our relationship with them.

Favoritism was definitely a factor between Rebekah and her sons. Esau was an outdoor type of guy who would have given an ancient Dick's Sporting Goods store a ton of business. Apparently, Isaac, his father, favored Esau for this and for the scrumptious steak he could whip up. Rebekah, however, favored her other son, Jacob, because he was the son who stayed home with her.

On top of this we learn from Genesis 26:34–35 that Esau married two foreign wives, which was a big whammy. In fact, verse 35 says that his wives "were a source of grief to Isaac and Rebekah." Sometimes our children or other people can wound us deeply, which also causes friction and distance in our relationships.

There was also one mega-prophecy that is important to note. When Rebekah was pregnant with the twin boys, she felt them struggling against each other in her womb. So she asked the Lord to help her understand why this was happening. The Lord responded that two nations would come from her babies. These nations would be divided against each other. More specifically, "one people will be stronger than the other, and the older will serve the younger" (Gen. 25:23). This would have been radical to hear back then, since the reverse was often true.

It's doubtful that Rebekah would have forgotten this, so seeing that Esau was about to receive the blessing, Rebekah may have panicked and figured she'd better help God fulfill prophecy. Or maybe it was out of offense or because of her deep love for Jacob that Rebekah was prompted to take matters into her own hands. Regardless, she deceived her husband, secured the blessing for Jacob, and then exclaimed that the Lord should put the curse of her actions directly upon her (Gen. 27:13)! What? And I thought using Butt Paste on my children sounded weird. I just don't get why she did this—like a modern mama whipping up a bouquet garni to throw into a stew. Calling a curse upon oneself is not something moms, or women in general, do today.

Or do we?

Here's an example of a woman who had total disregard for whatever pain or consequences would come upon her for her actions. Rebekah wanted what she wanted for her favorite son and that was that. I can also relate to wanting what I want, whether it be in my own life or for the lives of my children. Sometimes I grow impatient and disregard what the consequences of my actions could entail, trying to control things so that what I want to happen, happens.

However, the issues of impatience, setting high expectations, or needing to control things or people is not limited to women in the throes of motherhood. I realize that some of you reading this book may not be mothers, or you may have adult children who have left your home. Still, consider if you struggle with any of these things when relating to friends or family members or those in your workplace. Do you show favoritism or fall prey to falsely promoting yourself or manipulating to get your way? We gals, no matter our age or stage of life, can act like Rebekah if we're not vigilant. I know I struggled in several of these areas before I married and became a mother.

But now that I am a mom, my desire to provide the best for my kiddos or my desire for them to excel at life is, well . . . strong. So I tend to put expectations on myself and onto my kids that may not be fair. It's like I expect us to be picture-perfect and I become easily frustrated at myself, them, and God when things aren't that way.

The desire to control and manipulate rises up within my mama's heart, just like it did in Rebekah's. And while I may not be literally calling down a curse upon myself, my anger and frustration damages my relationships and unnecessarily punishes those I love as well.

Yep, definitely a mom fail.

Letting Distress Draw You Closer to God's Love

> Her husband Elkanah would say to her, "Hannah, why are you weeping? Why don't you eat? Why are you downhearted? Don't I mean more to you than ten sons?"
>
> Once when they had finished eating and drinking in Shiloh, Hannah stood up. Now Eli the priest was sitting on his chair by the doorpost of the LORD's house. In her deep anguish Hannah prayed to the LORD, weeping bitterly. And she made a vow, saying, "LORD Almighty, if you will only look on your servant's misery and remember me, and not forget your servant but give her a son, then I will give him to the LORD for all the days of his life, and no razor will ever be used on his head." (1 Sam. 1:8–11)

Now let's take a peek at the heart of Hannah, another mother mentioned in the Old Testament. Having children seemed like it would never happen for her, so when we meet Hannah we find her weeping and vowing to give her son back to the Lord and into his service should he give her one. Talk about a mom win.

Hannah's heart was surrendered, reverent, and thankful. If you read her prayer in 1 Samuel 2, you can tell that Hannah loved God. Here was a mother who knew her God intimately and who believed in him wholeheartedly. Hannah did not let her distress separate her from God but allowed it to draw her closer to God.

God blessed Hannah with a son and she kept her vow to him in return. In the end, God gave Hannah two daughters and three more sons. But her firstborn, Samuel, grew into a godly and influential leader of the nation of Israel.

Are We Driven by a Desire to Control or Motivated by Reverence?

Let's consider the contrast between Hannah and Rebekah. One mother deceived, while the other mother was transparent. Rebekah turned to her own plan to help her son, while Hannah let go of her plans, releasing her son into the capable hands of God. One mother wanted worldly blessings for her son, while the other mother wanted her son to serve and bless others. Rebekah called down a curse upon herself, while Hannah prayed blessing and praises back to God. The contrast between these two mothers is obvious.

Hannah knew her God and lived out her pop of color well. How I long for my heart to be like Hannah's and to live out my emphasis as a mother in a way that glorifies God. I desire to hold my children loosely and to remember that helping them to live their lives in service to God is more important than making them excel at all the things, achieve popularity, or have spotless rooms and a perfect GPA. If God has some of these things in his designs for them, great. If not, I am starting to see that this is also wonderful.

While Rebekah was driven by manipulation, Hannah was motivated by reverence. Whenever my mama's heart is ruled by wanting to control or romancing unrealistic expectations, I too must assume a posture of reverence and submission, remembering who my God is and that I am not him. Hannah's example is challenging me to let go of who I think my children should be. She inspires me to truly release them to God, listening and watching as he molds them into who he wants them to be. And on the days when how I act toward them contrasts with the way God desires for me to act toward them, I'm quicker to confess and correct myself and try again.

In fact, the other day I was talking with my friend Shontell about this very thing. She shared that early on in her own season of motherhood, she viewed raising her children as more of a burden instead of a blessing. Similar to the apostle Paul, God captured her attention somewhere along a proverbial road in Nevada (instead of Damascus) and revealed to her how her mama's heart was becoming blurred with selfishness. Shontell also gave me permission to share the following with you:

> I've never read about a more contrasting situation than the life of Paul, once Saul. I may not have had an extreme conversion like he did (murderer to God's spokesperson), but there was a time I went to bed with one set of thoughts and woke up a changed person altogether. No longer was I going to plan according to what I wanted. I was going to live according to God's call for my life: being a wife and mama. I vowed to change my tune to worship God in thanks for the opportunity to borrow these tiny humans. I felt like Wonder Woman realizing I have a lasso, armor strong enough to ward off bullets, and an invisible plane. I could see clearly for the first time in ages, and I knew

God was calling me to bring a new message about the beautiful mission of motherhood to those around me.

~Shontell Brewer

Our jobs, our possessions, our friends and families are all on loan from God and are parts of our redesigned life.

Shontell went on to share this new message in a book appropriately titled *Missionary Mom*. How I love watching God redesign the emphasis of my friend's life. There really are no small parts for us to play in God's plans for our lives.

Like Shontell, I am putting on glasses of surrender and looking through new lenses of reverence and release. I'm giving my children and their futures back to God, because he knows what is best for them. They're simply on loan from him to me to love and steward well. This is so freeing! They will probably do something opposite of what I hoped for in some way—which is not always a bad thing but most certainly a God thing.

If you're reading this and you're not a mother or in the same season of motherhood that I am, consider how you can put on glasses of surrender and lenses of reverence and release in your current stage of life. Our jobs, our possessions, our friends and families are all on loan from God and are parts of our redesigned life. Which means any one of these things will probably end up being opposite of what you hoped for in some way too. This is okay—and again, by design.

Breaking Free of the Fake and Embracing Your Reality

Is there anything in your life that is turning out to be exactly opposite of what you hoped for? I encourage you to admit this and to never love a wordly ideal more than the reality of who you are. The same idea pertains to your child, friend, coworker, or your life in general. Your Ideal = God. No one is perfect except God himself. And none of us live a perfect life either. If we did, why would we think we would need God for anything?

The truth is, we will never find healing or joy when life doesn't go as planned if we deceive and cover up or pretend that all is well when it is not and we are not. Fight the temptation to falsely promote yourself or your children online or to those you are in community with. Be real. There is contrast in us all. This is by design.

In order to break the fake habit in your life:

Fight the temptation to falsely promote yourself or your children. Be real. There is contrast in us all. This is by design.

- *Lean into and learn from contrast.* Do not cover up, but 'fess up and fix up. Be honest and confess your sin. But don't beat yourself up, because Christ was beaten for you. There's no condemnation for those who place their faith in Jesus Christ, just lots of beautiful sanctification instead.

- *Allow the lens of God's Word and the gift of account-ability in community to help you see and live clearer and truer.* You may be surprised at what happens when you let the rest of us get to know and love the real you. Yes, there may be some who reject or critique you. But there will be many more who identify with and will be inspired by you. For God is busy redesigning their life too. Remind them of this. Be someone's Hannah.

135

- *Resist the temptation to blend in or camouflage with our culture.* Clothe yourself in the complementary virtues of Christ by putting on the truths and promises of Scripture. You are couture and created to pop. Stand on the principles and patterns found in the Bible in order to do so. Do not place your trust in the mantra of a fallible, earthly guru, but on the promises of an infallible, divine God.

While cooking or parenting mishaps can make for some humorous social media posts, fails of the heart—often the ones we keep secret—are not that funny. Unique and beloved children of God embrace the reality of who they are and do not cover up the contrast that is happening within them. When it comes to living life with our people, I encourage you to choose honesty and grace over deceit and offense. Release expectations of perfectionism whether they are directed at you or at others, and seek to show love to everyone, even when they offend you or are different from you. I know this isn't the way of the world, but it is the way of Yahweh. And it is why God is using contrast to redesign your life.

Let's end this chapter in prayer, asking God to help us love our own Esau, friend, or coworker. For as we will see in the next chapter, when things are wobbly within our hearts, we may be off balance and headed for a fall.

Lord, help me to have a heart like Hannah's. How often I want to look pulled together and perfect. But you see the real me and you love me anyway. Forgive me of my pride and for my attempts to control or expect perfection from myself and from those I love. You are Perfection, God; fill me with more of you so I do not seek from those around me the things that only you can give. Help me to truly win in this life in ways that bring you honor and glory. Do what you want with the precious people and gifts you have given me to enjoy. Amen.

Muse Minutes

1. To help cement principle #4 into that beautiful mind and heart of yours, rewrite in your own words what *contrast* is here.

   Rewrite in your own words how God uses this principle in our lives.

2. As followers of Christ, the level of contrast between what we used to be and who we are now should become more evident as the years pass. Have you seen this to be true in your own life? List two or three specific examples here. Or ask a close friend, family member, or spouse what differences or contrast they notice in you.

3. Has God brought into your life people who think
   or act differently than you do, or has he brought
   circumstances into your life that played out opposite
   of what you wanted? Why do you think he did so,
   and how did you learn or grow from these things or
   people? Ask God to show you if there is any sin or
   unrealistic expectation clouding your vision right
   now. What is he showing you?

DESIGN TIP
for Your Home and Heart

We have different gifts, according to the grace given to each of us. (Rom. 12:6)

I am often asked, does everything in my home have to match? Sometimes the person asking means color-wise, and other times they mean style-wise. My answer is no! Your furniture pieces do not have to be the same shade of blue. In fact, it is nearly impossible to get the fabric, carpet color, and paint to be the same shade of a particular color. Contrast is a good thing, and varying shades of a color throughout a room is too.

Regarding style, just because your home is mostly done in a contemporary style doesn't mean you can't have an antique side table or chair thrown into the mix. Adding a piece that is from a different style or time period adds interest to the space.

This made me think of you and me. Sometimes we don't feel stylish or that we belong. We may be all *contemporary* and everyone else is, well . . . *traditional*. I encourage you to be you. We are not created to match everyone else's style. Varying spiritual gifts and talents have been given to all of us, which creates beauty and interest within the kingdom of God. He has placed you where you are for a reason. Eclectic is in, so embrace how God has made you and whatever room he has seated you in.

lance

nine

Experiencing Perfect Stability with God

I recently watched a movie about a man who walked across an itty-bitty wire that was secured between the Twin Towers of the original World Trade Center in New York City. On August 7, 1974, Philippe Petit stepped out onto the high wire, balance pole in hand, and took a step. And then he took another bunch of delicate steps all the way across the 140-foot wire to the North Tower. Then he went back and forth between the North and South Towers eight times before stopping. Talk about a man whose very life depended on the importance of balance! There was no safety net below him. If Philippe had lost his balance, that would have been the end for him. But he planned, practiced, and risked much to achieve his goal.

Unfortunately, officials at the World Trade Center did not rejoice with Philippe. Police were waiting for the daredevil to finish his death-defying jaunt in the sky, arresting him immediately as he finished. In the end, all charges against Philippe were dropped and he became a hero. "*Time* magazine called the high-wire act the 'artistic crime of the century.' Even the owners of the World Trade Center forgave Petit and gave him a lifetime pass to the observation deck."[1]

How I love to watch the courage and forgiveness of others become part of history. Petit clearly trespassed and did something crazy. While World Trade Center officials had a right to press charges, they forgave him and then blessed him with a lifetime pass so he could enjoy the spot where he fulfilled his dream. This too should be applauded, for it seems that the world is becoming less and less peaceful, giving, and forgiving. Our relationships are off balance. I believe that God desires for them to be harmonious or balanced.

So while we would probably never attempt to walk across a tiny wire high above New York City, it may feel as if we are walking on a figurative tightrope some days, trying to find some sort of balance not only within ourselves, but in our relationships as well. And when things are wobbly within our hearts, we are at risk of falling or doing something that injures us and those around us. In a spiritual sense we may also be pushing God away intentionally or unintentionally.

Is relational and spiritual balance, like physical balance, possible? Yes, I believe it is. I believe it to be possible not only within our communities and homes, but also within our hearts. Ridding ourselves of whatever is causing us to wobble and loving God and those around us carefully is key to maintaining an inward and outward sense of balance as we uncover the purposes of God whenever life doesn't go as we planned.

Balance: The Division of Visual Weight

Presenting a vista to the viewer that offers different areas of equal interest to the eye is what balance is all about. This means bringing equilibrium or stability to the space.[2]

Balance is another fundamental design principle. There are three types of balance: symmetrical, asymmetrical, and radial. Radial balance is the least occurring of the three. It has elements extending outward from a central point. Think of a flower, bicycle wheel, or chandelier as examples of items that embody radial balance.

Symmetrical balance occurs when everything looks "even" size- and number-wise from a visual standpoint. This is the most stable type of balance. However, too much symmetry can make a space or work of art feel repetitive or dull.

Asymmetrical balance allows for a little more creativity, making the room or piece of art feel more exciting, active, or informal than a symmetrically balanced one. Not every element in the design has to be of the same size, shape, or quantity throughout the artwork or room. However, if some sense of balance is not achieved or if the elements do not appear to equal each other visually, the painting will feel off or the room will feel disorganized and uninviting. Thus, the influence of this principle is felt in an accessory, artwork, or architectural standpoint in design.

Pause for a moment and Google "classical architecture." Take a look at the structures done in the classical style. This type of architecture employs a lot of balanced symmetry, giving ancient temples or buildings a more stately and formal vibe.

The White House in Washington, DC, is one of the more familiar examples of a building done in classical-style architecture here in the United States. The main door is smack-dab in the middle of the house. If you were to draw a line down the center of the main entryway, you would find the same number of windows on either side of the imaginary line, giving the exterior façade a balanced feeling. On the south side of the White House is the Truman Balcony and the south portico. These are placed in the center of the building. The six columns supporting the roof above these areas are evenly spaced with three columns placed on either side of the middle of the balcony and the portico. This is the essence of symmetrical balance.

Or picture in your mind a brick fireplace and its wooden mantel. Oh happy day, you get to venture out to your nearest Target, where you end up finding some really cute picture frames and decorative candles that would make Joanna Gaines swoon. Then you return home and start to arrange them on your mantel.

If you place one silver frame and one white candle on the left side of your mantel, and then place the remaining silver frame and white candle on the right side of your mantel, you are incorporating the principle of symmetrical balance into your design. Both ends of the mantel contain the same size, color, and quantity of objects. Everything looks balanced and even.

Now go back to imagining a simple brick fireplace and its wooden mantel again. If you were to rearrange the picture frames and decorative candles you bought at Target, placing one of the picture frames and two candles on one side of the mantel, and leaving one picture frame by itself on the other end of the mantel, then you are now using asymmetrical balance in your design.

Thus, balance is essentially based on visual weight and its distribution within an interior room or piece of artwork. If the balance of anything is off, it will not look or feel right. The same is true of our hearts. This is by design. God allows us to feel off balance whenever there is something wrong in our hearts or in our relationships or careers. We plan to be the perfect friend and plan on being loved by perfect friends in return. Or we intend to be the perfect employee, boss, or church volunteer. And then drama happens. And the warm fuzzy sentiment we feel toward someone disappears.

Then there is our relationship with God. Things usually feel smooth between him and us when life is awesome. But when life shocks or disappoints and we beg God to make things right or like what we had originally wanted or intended but he is silent or says no, we may push him away or become angry at him, causing our relationship with God to feel off.

Take a quick assessment of your relationship with God and with others. Do these connections feel imbalanced at all? Do they feel strained? Why might this be so?

Since life doesn't remain the same for any of us, how we balance our relationship with God and with other people may look a little more asymmetrical than symmetrical at times— which is okay, because both are types of balance. In fact, our relationship with God will always be asymmetrical—we can never equal, outgive, or outlove God! And yet, as we learned in the chapter covering the principle of pattern, God still delights in what we do offer him since we are his beloved.

Similarly, there will be seasons when our human relationships feel asymmetrical as well, since sometimes we give more of our time and guidance to others than they are able to give back to us, and vice versa. Yet if we are truly loving our friends, coworkers, or family members, we won't be keeping score but extending them grace instead.

And then there are certain people who will only be a part of our life for a shorter season of time. You may be grieving the loss of a relationship that you thought would always be a part of your life. Know that my heart aches with yours over this. Nothing makes us wobble or completely fall over like a damaged or broken relationship. However, you are still loved. What separates you from someone else can never separate you from your God (Rom. 8:38–39). May God help you to rejoice over those who do remain in your life, and may he give you the strength to let go of the people who have left.

Reducing Drama by Disciplining Ourselves

Other things such as crisis, physical distance, time, or heart issues like unforgiveness or becoming numb to the things of God throw us off, negatively affecting the balance of our relationships with God and those around us. Forgiving others, showing grace, and remaining steadfast in our faith and friendships enable us to live a balanced life relationally and spiritually.

Similarly, practicing the spiritual disciplines also helps us free ourselves from the trappings of self-indulgence and from becoming off balance and throwing stones at others. As my friend, Anna, rightly points out, spiritual laziness prevents us from loving others as Jesus

Forgiving others, showing grace, and remaining steadfast in our faith and friendships enable us to live a balanced life relationally and spiritually.

has asked us to. The "road" is narrow indeed. Make sure you're on it.

Disciplining Ourselves along the Grace-Filled Path

Anna LeBaron

As believers, we journey in The Way of Christ that leads to abundant life. Matthew 7:14 reminds us, "But small is the gate and narrow the road that leads to life."

However, an imbalance occurs in our lives when we fall into the ditch on either side of this narrow road. On one side of the road we find a life wrought with the trappings of hedonism, a life centered upon the pursuit of pleasure and self-indulgence. On the other side is a life held in the stranglehold of legalism, an excessive adherence to formulas and activities that gives the outward appearance of a desired outcome but that leaves the inner being unchanged. Falling to either side and remaining there indefinitely have the potential to stall us out in our faith journey.

I have found myself stalled out in either ditch on several occasions, sometimes by my own doing and other times through no fault of mine. We have an enemy who loves nothing more than turning our focus on the wrong things, baiting us to take our eyes off the only thing that matters—becoming more like Christ.

We feel frustrated, realizing that our faith has become stagnant instead of deepening into the abundant life we were made to live. We are created for a life of forward movement along the grace-filled path, not a life slogging through ditches. The key to staying on the narrow path is practicing the disciplines of the Christian life.

Had we identified ourselves as disciples of Jesus during his lifetime, both our goal and desire would have been to follow so closely in his steps that we would become increasingly more like the teacher. The manner in which we lived our lives would emulate his in character and deed.

Through the ordinary disciplines of the Christian life, believers are responsible for doing the necessary, humanly possible things to stay on the narrow path. As we carry out these common, doable things, God accomplishes the impossible and our lives are transformed.

In fact, there are two types of spiritual disciplines. There are disciplines of abstinence like solitude, silence, fasting, frugality, chastity, secrecy, and sacrifice. There are also disciplines of engagement like study, worship, celebration, service, prayer, fellowship, confession, and submission.

By regularly practicing and engaging in the disciplines, we reflect his character so that those around us can experience the life of Christ through us. As a result, we exhibit the fruit of the Spirit: love, joy, peace, patience, kindness, goodness, faithfulness, gentleness, and self-control (Gal. 5:22–23 ESV). This reflection becomes an increasing, ongoing reality when the practice of the disciplines is evidenced in our lives.

Have you ever known someone who exhibits joy, peace, patience, or any of the other things that Anna mentioned? These are gifts from the Holy Spirit and are probably a result of that person engaging in some heavy-duty prayer time, worship, and study of the Scriptures.

Spiritual disciplines are another tool we use to help us remain in harmony with God and with others. There may be seasons when our use of the disciplines looks a little more asymmetrical than symmetrical and this is okay. There will be seasons when God calls us away from certain things or relationships in order for us to rest or draw closer to him via a time of fasting, prayer, and solitude.

Remember that spiritual laziness causes us to stray away from loving God and others as he intended. If we are not practicing some of the things that Anna mentioned, we will be off balance. So if any of these disciplines seem foreign to you or you've never tried them, do some reading up on them and, as God leads you, incorporate them into your daily routine.[3] Remaining steadfast in our faith enables us to live a balanced life relationally and spiritually, helping us draw closer to God and experience him more. This in turn helps us love those we're in community with in a way that benefits them and brings God glory.

Balance within the Pages of Scripture

As I mentioned in the previous chapter, having unrealistic expectations of others affects our relationships. Things like envy, jealousy, selfishness, pride, and gossip also cause relationships to weaken or collapse. While the Bible has much to say about issues like these, one of the biggest issues that causes us to lose our balance as we relate to others and to God is unforgiveness. This is tragic, especially since our God is a God of restoration and peace, and desires for us to be the same.

God's Restoration of and Forgiveness toward Us

We've all been saddened by the news of a breakup. Maybe it was your friend and her beau. Tom Cruise and Nicole Kidman.

NSYNC or the Spice Girls. I cannot stand fighting, drama, and division. Like, no. Everyone stop and hug right now and hold lit candles and sway back and forth together. Just saying. I am such a lover of balance in all relationships near and far forever and ever, amen.

And while I can't be sure if God is into lighting candles and swaying back and forth, I am positive he is into restoration and forgiveness. He is a God of balance, second chances, and peace (John 14:27; 1 Cor. 14:33; Phil. 4:9). Since his designs for us include interaction with him and with those around us, he desires for us to forgive and to live in peace so far as it is in our power to do so (Rom. 12:17–18). When we are at odds with others or holding a grudge, God allows us to feel off or imbalanced because our grudge outweighs the grace in our heart.

When we are at odds with others or holding a grudge, God allows us to feel off or imbalanced because our grudge outweighs the grace in our heart.

It's also important that we are at peace with God. Because of his love for us, God longs to restore us back into a right relationship with him. However, we often allow sin and things like laziness, doubt, unforgiveness, and busyness to take our focus off God, creating a wedge between us and him that wasn't part of our original state nor part of his original design for our lives.

There was no need for restoration or forgiveness before the fall of mankind. Life was perfect for Adam and Eve in the beginning. They experienced perfect stability in their relationship with God. But then they rebelled, sin entered the world, and the relationship between mankind and God was thrown off. I'm not saying that we have ever been on the same level with God in any way; we are the created, and he is the Creator. But originally there was peace and harmony between Adam, Eve, and God, so a figurative balance was experienced in their relationship before the fall. They had open and unashamed access to walk with God in the garden, naked. But then sin tipped the relational scales, so to speak. Their eyes were opened, they became aware of their nakedness, and they hid from God. And we've inherited the same tendency. Are you hiding from God today?

Pause and consider for a moment if you are at peace with God. Do you see him as a Father or as a foe? Are you blaming him for something, forgetting that he is neither the source nor the cause of evil in this world? If you are feeling that God is distant or that he is against you, it could be because you are harboring some disappointment, doubt, or unforgiveness toward God in your heart. God knows how you're really feeling, but he still loves you and wants to be with you. Be encouraged—he's just waiting for you to talk to him about it.

Come clean, child of God. Give God your gunk and grudge(s). Your God is a mighty God who can handle the realness and weight of your frustrations and doubts. Lay these before him in prayer, as many times as it takes. Do not stuff the anger or the unforgiveness. Like Adam and Eve, come out from behind whatever "bush" you are hiding behind and allow God to take the feelings or the circumstances that are causing you to waver. Give God time to fill you with his peace, perspective, and grace so that your relationship with him can be restored once again.

Our Restoration and Forgiveness of Others

God not only desires for us to be at peace with him but with each other as well since we are all made in his image. One of the ways to achieve this is to model the forgiveness of God toward those who have wronged you, either intentionally or unintentionally. Forgiveness lightens your heart and your spirit. It helps you to heal and move forward. It does not mean you approve or are even happy about what happened. Forgiveness doesn't automatically rewind time, make us forget our hurt, or magically repair or return what was damaged or lost. Please understand that I'm not advocating for us to forgive and then place ourselves back into a situation where we are abused physically, sexually, emotionally, or spiritually.

Sometimes damage really does occur. And sometimes there are consequences or discipline that needs to happen as a result of what our offender has done to us. Matthew 18 does set a precedent for church discipline. And remember the heavy truth we looked at in the last chapter: our God cannot stand sin. Therefore, we can trust that ultimate justice for the wrongs done to us or those we love will be carried out by God in the end (Rom. 12:19). So, yes, there are times when there will be consequences. However, God will ultimately carry that out, and he still extends forgiveness to us. Therefore, we should extend it to others. Here are snippets of what the Bible says about forgiveness:

We forgive others because Christ first forgave us.

Get rid of all bitterness, rage and anger, brawling and slander, along with every form of malice. Be kind and compassionate to one another, forgiving each other, just as in Christ God forgave you. (Eph. 4:31–32)

God's forgiveness toward us is limitless. Therefore, we aim to forgive others as many times as needed.

For as high as the heavens are above the earth,
    so great is his love for those who fear him;

as far as the east is from the west,
so far has he removed our transgressions from us.
(Ps. 103:11–12)

If we do not forgive, then God will not forgive us.

For if you forgive other people when they sin against you, your heavenly Father will also forgive you. But if you do not forgive others their sins, your Father will not forgive your sins. (Matt. 6:14–15)

Pretty sobering verses, aren't they? Forgiveness is a big deal. Next time your relationship with God or with someone in your life feels off, check to see if unforgiveness is an issue. If it is, give your grudge into the hands of your gracious God. Ask him to help you let go of the offense and hurt and to see the offender as he would have you see them. Yes, this is hard. As I wrote this chapter, the Lord revealed several people I needed to forgive. Here is an example of a prayer I pray to help me do so. If you are stuck in a rut of unforgiveness, personalizing Bible verses and praying through them will help you let go and move forward.

Father God, I thank you for giving us an example of how to pray in your Word. My heart is hurting and I am struggling to forgive those who have hurt me. I pray for your kingdom to come and I ask for your will to be done in my life and in the lives of those I am having trouble forgiving (Luke 11:2). Help me to love them and to know the best way to interact with them going forward. Give me the strength to let go of the hurt and offense that is within my heart and forgive me of my own sins today, Father God (Luke 11:4). Thank you for providing for all my needs and for meeting with me here (Luke 11:3). I pray this in the power of your Son Jesus's name. Amen.

Diminish the Drama

Let's return to looking at the life of King David as we end this chapter. We know from reading the Psalms that David had a lot of enemies. One of them happened to be his predecessor, King Saul. In the beginning of their relationship, all was well. David soothed Saul with his musical skills, and all seemed balanced between them. But over time, Saul allowed the jealousy and contempt he felt toward David to throw his heart off balance. And then Saul sought to kill David, whom he used to favor. Talk about drama! And we think it's cruel when someone unfollows us on Twitter or unfriends us on Facebook. Ha. *This is drama*, and because of it, Saul and David's relationship was never restored.

This is why letting go of offense within our heart diminishes drama. God desires for us to be free and full of peace, love, and grace. He does not desire for us to be ruled by bitterness, offense, or anger. Harboring both love and offense in our heart causes us to lose our balance. Trying to extend genuine grace and patience to others from one side of our heart, while allowing bitterness to remain on the other side of our heart, will not work. We will be imbalanced.

This is why it is so important to pay attention to how we are feeling as we relate

Trying to extend genuine grace and patience to others from one side of our heart, while allowing bitterness to remain on the other side of our heart, will not work. We will be imbalanced.

to God and others. We have got to nip jealousy or unforgiveness in the bud ASAP. Otherwise it will fester and grow, and we will wobble. There are some who make light of emotions or believe we should dismiss them entirely. I disagree. Yes, they can deceive us at times (Jer. 17:9), but we still need to acknowledge them because they affect how we treat others and how we relate to God.

Drama affects distribution. Replaying drama in our hearts and minds throws us further off balance and affects our ability to effectively distribute our time, love, or help to those around us. So take some time to assess your relationships. God uses the principle of balance as an indicator of our physical, emotional, and spiritual well-being for a reason. Without balance we will fall, and with it we can love and live out our redesigned life well. So practice the spiritual disciplines regularly and diminish the drama by forgiving and pursuing reconciliation with God and others.

Even if we never walk across a teeny-tiny wire above the streets of New York, we will literally walk into a friend's home, or walk figuratively within our online communities or circles. Make sure that everything within you is balanced.

ten

Loving Others Un-conditionally

As I said before, my life turned into a USAA TV commercial, and I became a moving-all-over-the-place military spouse and mother of two. One of the things affected by these special and beautiful callings was my friendships. When I was single I felt like I was able to balance working, me time, and time with friends. But moving all over the country makes finding and keeping friendships almost impossible. Having babies also makes it difficult to find time to shower, let alone be awake enough to love your girlfriends well. Now my babies are older and are involved in all of the school things. On top of their activities, I still have my ministry and all my online friends and readers to love on. Some days I still feel unable to balance doing all the things and loving all my people well.

Maybe life has surprised you and you're living in a place you swore you'd never live. So you find yourself opening your home and heart to new people when you'd rather keep hanging out with those you've known for years. Or what about your best bud at work or church who left or moved away? And what about your gal pal who is saving the world with flawless makeup and perfect offspring while your kids are struggling in school and you can barely make it out of bed? Let's face it, loving people with a smile on the outside *and* inside of us is sometimes hard.

But what I am learning is that hundreds of miles, the ministry success of our bestie, perfect Instagram images, or motherhood itself does not have to hinder our relationships. For example, I have been through a lot with my friend Jenet over the years. We did youth ministry together, were in each other's weddings, and became moms around the same time. Yet Jenet and I have lived in different cities, and mostly different states, throughout the entirety of my marriage.

The distance between us hasn't been a detriment. Jenet remains one of my most loyal and supportive friends. We say the hard things to one another. We have varying interests, so our ministries look different. Jenet is more introspective, and, well, I am just *intro* nothing but *out there* with everything instead. We've gone through loss, celebrations, and hormonal changes together. Weeks can go by before we chat again, and we are okay with this. I am never too much or never not enough for her. Even though we do not get to see each other in person that often, we use FaceTime or Marco Polo to help ease all the "missing you" moments in between seeing one another in person.

God has taught us much over the years. One of the biggest things he taught us over the summer of 2011 was to keep our friendship in perspective. Earlier that year, my husband and I had been planning a trip overseas. We were going to drop our kids off at their grandparents' house and then head out of town for our adventure. On the way into Phoenix, my phone rang. It was Jenet, who was frantic. Her husband had come down with bacterial meningitis, winding up in a medically induced coma. It wasn't looking good. Jenet was also seven months pregnant with their second child at the time. She was overwhelmed and extra tired, and I was desperate to get to her, thinking the coincidence of us driving into Phoenix—which is where she lives—was such a gift.

But I never got to hold my friend's hand that day or during the days that followed. I remained apart from her, holding my iPhone with her on the other end of it instead. Days prior to our arriving in Phoenix, I had been sick. I was still not feeling 100 percent, so per hospital rules I was not allowed to go near the ICU and sit with my friend. Jenet and I were devastated. At one point I pleaded with Chad to cancel our trip. How could I leave my best friend behind and enjoy our time away? What if her husband died? I felt I could never forgive myself for leaving her if he did.

But it was too late for us to change our plans. Jenet understood, and we shed some tears on the phone as we said goodbye. The flight over the ocean and the first couple days of the trip felt heavy whenever my thoughts wandered back to Jenet. I had no idea what was happening with her or if my best friend had become a widow. On Cinco de Mayo, Jenet's husband woke up from his coma. And in early August, Jenet delivered a healthy baby boy. Her husband continues to remain healthy and they have added a little girl to their family.

I'm grateful for all that God has done in the life of this family, although I do not understand why the meningitis had to happen in the first place. What I do know is that I watched my friend's faith grow stronger since this crisis occurred. But initially Jenet and I could not understand why I was the only one who was not allowed inside the hospital room that day. And why I had to be an ocean apart from my dearest friend when she needed me the most.

I do wonder though if I had been there with Jenet, would she have cried out to God as much as she ended up doing? Or would she have cried just to me? Would we have leaned on each other more than our God in those moments of worry and fear? Probably. Because we are human. But this would have made us imbalanced. What Jenet and I learned that summer was that our God could and would be there for us when we could not be there for each other. This incident has helped us to develop a habit of running to God first to be filled up, before running to each other, and that's helped us to remain balanced relationally with him and with one another.

Let's look at one last snapshot from King David's life. David not only loved God, he loved his friend Jonathan too. And yet we know from looking at the totality of what was written in the Psalms by David that God, not Jonathan, was the focal point of David's life. Even though David was supported and loved by Jonathan, David still found his ultimate strength and protection in God and not in his friend. And since David was on the run from his enemies, he probably didn't get much face time with his dear friend either. But he was able to maintain heart time with God while on the run, which is what kept David balanced and steadfast.

There Is Room for All of Us

> After David had finished talking with Saul, Jonathan became
> one in spirit with David, and he loved him as himself. From
> that day Saul kept David with him and did not let him return
> home to his family. And Jonathan made a covenant with David
> because he loved him as himself. Jonathan took off the robe he
> was wearing and gave it to David, along with his tunic, and even
> his sword, his bow and his belt. (1 Sam. 18:1–4)

Okay, so we typically do not make covenants with our friends
these days. But we may gift each other with a cappuccino or
some cute Kate Spade earrings or something. In David's day,
covenants were more common and were often public events,
signaling that the two parties involved were now sworn brothers
for life. By placing his robe upon David and by giving him parts
of his military dress, Jonathan bestowed on David one of the
highest honors in the land. In other words, this was a big deal.

What a different man Jonathan was from his father, Saul.
While Saul was threatened by David's rising popularity and
military victories, Jonathan grew in his respect for David,
rightly recognizing that God's anointing was upon him. The
two became friends, had a mutual respect, and swore their love
and loyalty to one another.

Several times their commitment to one another was tested,
but the friends remained true to their word. Sadly, Jonathan
died in battle, apart from David. I bet you anything David
wished he could've been there to protect his friend. Maybe
David mourned the fact he was unable to hold Jonathan's hand
in that final moment. All David had left were memories of his
friend and perhaps Jonathan's robe or bow to hold instead
of his hand. This reminds me of our smartphones with their

pictures and videos of our loved ones. Our phone may be all we have left to hold when we would rather be holding the other person's hand.

Life is precious and so is friendship. I pray we would not let drama ruin things. At some point we are all going to meet a David. To others we will *be* a David. We can choose to celebrate the other person, recognizing that prior to their success and popularity they may have been in a season of obscurity like David when he was out in the pastures, unnoticed and just a simple shepherd boy. They've probably fought their share of Goliaths like David too.

There really is room enough around the table of God for all of us. God allowed four Gospel accounts to be included in the accepted canon of the Bible, did he not? Which means four different men with four different perspectives got to add their unique view so the picture of Jesus's life and ministry could be more complete. As I said, there really is enough room for all of us to use our talents and testimonies to benefit the kingdom of God.

We cannot hold both love and hate together in our heart. Doing so causes us to lose balance. Only love can bring balance to our lives. And love looks a whole lot like celebrating the accomplishments of others, extending grace, and resting in the beauty and significance of our own emphasis. As we saw with Jonathan and David, we must love others as we love ourselves so we can be relationally balanced. This is the ultimate

> Only love can bring balance to our lives. And love looks a whole lot like celebrating the accomplishments of others, extending grace, and resting in the beauty and significance of our own emphasis.

way and one of the greatest commandments in the entire Bible (Matt. 22:36–40; see also 1 Cor. 13).

Speaking of the Bible, my friend Bobbie has seen the Scriptures help her stay balanced spiritually and relationally. Now when she is tempted to use harsh words or nurse negative attitudes toward those she is in relationship with, she knows how to regain her balance and love like a Jonathan. Bobbie says:

> Balance has always been hard for me. It isn't just physical balance that I struggle with. I've struggled with spiritual balance as well. I'd start my days with determination and poise, but by the end of my day, I'd sway and collide with the people around me.
>
> I haven't quite figured out a way to improve my balance physically, but I do know what has helped me keep balanced in my spiritual life. The truths of God's Word have always been the steady ground that I could stand on when things started to shift and veer out of my control. Now I bring myself back in balance as often as I need to by reflecting on and applying the biblical truths I read. I'm falling into things like harsh words, negative attitudes, and other sin less often because I balance on the steadfast truth in the Word of God. God's Word is the only solid ground we have to stand on. When you start to sway and lean, let it bring you back into balance.
>
> ~Bobbie Schaeperkoetter

God's Word is the solid ground on which we can and must stand. So let's continually turn to it and let Scripture bring our hearts and minds back into balance. As Bobbie mentioned, we need the Word of God to steady us and help us remove whatever sin or negative attitudes exist in our hearts, for these will cause our relationships with others and with God to become unstable. Let the words of your God stabilize you whenever you start to sway.

Loving Others Unconditionally

Even though God wants us to be in community with those around us, we sometimes become unbalanced, running the risk of depending on others more than we depend on him. Then, when we find the person or people we depend on the most are unavailable to help us, we fall apart. Instead of getting upset or frustrated at them or at God for this, let's see these opportunities as a little reminder of who our ultimate strength and comfort is. Our friends, coworkers, and family members cannot ultimately comfort or fulfill our every need. They weren't created to be an all-red room and neither were we. So give them grace.

Here are some tips to help you love others in an unconditional and balanced way:

We truly have no idea of the battles, physical or emotional, the people in our lives have fought through to get to where they are now.

- *Re-gift grace.* Instead of throwing rocks of jealousy, gossip, or indifference toward a David in our life, we should extend them the grace they deserve. God has given us the gift of grace, has he not? We must seize opportunities to do the same for those around us. We truly have no idea of the battles, physical or emotional, the people in our lives have fought through to get to where they are now, whatever success looks like for them.

- *Rid your heart of idols.* If we start to idolize someone, thinking they're perfect and can do no wrong, we fall prey to focusing only on their positives, forgetting they need a Savior just like the rest of us do. Idolization causes imbalance. So be careful not to turn to those you admire for affirmation and/or strength. God is the only perfect, ultimate source of whatever it is we are needing. Our friends and family were not created to be fillers or our focus. God is to be the focal point of our life. If a relationship becomes imbalanced, it could be part of God's movement to turn your focus back to him.

- *Refocus on God!* You and I are his beloved and anointed by him to fulfill his designs for our lives. Thus, we should praise God for our friends and for the blessings that are happening in their lives. Otherwise we may become envious of the way they look, their ministry, their house, or their family and let jealousy and bitterness eat us alive and damage the relationship.

Give your grudges to God and remember that holding relationships loosely, cultivating constant forgiveness, and loving others unconditionally helps you maintain balance within your relationships and within your heart. Cling tightly to your creative Creator before all else so that if you are holding an iPhone instead of a friend's hand, you'll be able to feel content, knowing that you loved them like a Jonathan would. It's certain that as we continue to walk across the figurative tightrope of life we will lose someone or something we love.

As we head into the final principle section of this book, I want you to think about how precious life really is. I imagine you've experienced the death of something, whether it be a dream or a loved one. Maybe a certain something was supposed to happen, or a certain someone is supposed to be here with you. But your dream or loved one died. As you are about to see, God is close to the brokenhearted. The hole that loss has left in your heart can be filled again. Even this is by design.

Muse Minutes

1. To help cement principle #5 into that beautiful mind and heart of yours, rewrite in your own words what *balance* is here.

   Rewrite in your own words how God uses this principle in our lives.

2. Do you see God as a Father or as a foe? Are you blaming him for something, forgetting that God is neither the source nor the cause of evil in this world? Do you believe God is for you or against you? Explain.

3. Is forgiveness something that is easy or difficult for you? Why do you think this is?

If forgiveness is difficult for you, what are some things that may help you grow in your ability to forgive God or others more easily? (I encourage you to pray and talk to God about these. Ask him to help you forgive as he forgives. I also encourage you to share your answers with someone who is trustworthy so they can be praying for and encouraging you in this area of your life.)

DESIGN TIP

for Your Home and Heart

Therefore each of you must put off falsehood and speak truthfully to your neighbor, for we are all members of one body. (Eph. 4:25)

Wish you had a bigger home, but your season of life or budget will not allow it? Try this trick. Larger mirrors create an illusion that makes an interior space feel bigger than it is. Most of my clients wanted bigger spaces to move around in, but since they didn't have the budget to knock down walls or install more windows, I suggested hanging mirrors to create the illusion that the space was bigger than it was.

However, while you may want to hang some mirrors on your walls, there's no room for illusion within your relationships. God wants us to be honest with one another. Fight the temptation to hide behind a mirror that distorts who you are in order to be accepted or validated. Choose integrity over illusion. Rest in how God has designed you to be—one of a kind.

Space

eleven

Filling Yourself with God as You Grieve

Death rarely inconvenienced me or made its presence known in my life while I was growing up. I'd always heard about death, of course, and knew it was something that happens to all of us. I had friends lose someone they loved, and my great-grandparents passed away when I was a little girl. But for the most part I didn't give death much thought until it came time for the woman I loved most in this world to experience it.

I watched my mother slowly die over a span of eleven years. It was as if her bags were symbolically packed for heaven, sitting quietly over in the corner of the room, staring at me. I rode the roller coaster of emotions, thinking she was close to dying, then watching her recover and suffer some more. My mother was even placed into hospice care only to rebound and return home with us a couple of days later. Her bags remained packed for another two months.

On October 8, 2012, my mother was fully healed in heaven. I'd give anything to still have her here. She is supposed to be helping me raise my children and cheering me on as I write this book. But my mother is dead. And now her bags are gone.

Loss of any kind leaves an empty, negative space in our hearts. But God has a purpose for this, and he uses it to fill us with what is positive.

> Loss of any kind leaves an empty, negative space in our hearts. But God has a purpose for this, and he uses it to fill us with what is positive.

Space: The Occupied or Empty Places in or around a Masterpiece

Space in art refers to the distance or area between, around, above, below, or within shapes and forms found within a composition.

Positive space is the "occupied" areas in a work of art that is filled with something such as lines, colors and shapes.

Negative space is the unoccupied areas that surround the subject matter. . . . It goes in all directions and goes on forever.[1]

We have arrived at our last design principle. This one is probably the hardest to grasp or is the most abstract one of them all, but space is a critical yet overlooked thing to consider whenever we design or create anything. The important thing to remember is that negative space primarily draws our attention back to the positive space in a room, on the printed page, or in a piece of art.

For example, the designer for the interior of this book understands and utilized positive and negative space to design this page. Notice there is less space between the individual letters in these words so you can read and decipher what they mean. Also note how there is more space between the paragraphs or between the entire chapters of this book, which also helps you understand where a complete group of thoughts ends and begins. Think what would happen if the designer undermined the importance of the negative space and filled the whole page with words without leaving any space between them!

Or think what would happen if someone who designs plastic containers disregarded this principle. For them to make a useful product, they must first consider how big or small the objects (the positive space) are that will be placed within the interior of the container (the negative space). If they disregard the positive space, the negative space may not be able to store the things it was designed to hold. Positive space influences negative space.

The same is true for our homes. If the space within a home is filled to the brim, it feels cluttered and dirtier. Larger, more open spaces that have fewer items in them give one's mind and eyes a moment to pause. They can make a home feel roomier and cleaner. This is why I used to tell my clients that the cliché "less is more" really is true.

Likewise, grief and loss create their own type of silence or empty, negative space within our hearts. Grief is like negative space in a piece of art. It gives our life definition, and at times seems to go on forever, leaving its presence all over our actions and thoughts. Our grief, with its accompanying anger, depression, and fear, can feel like it is lord over us. Be encouraged, for it is not. God is sovereign and Lord over all of these things.

God, then, uses loss like an artist uses negative space to give us permission to pause, reevaluate, and ultimately draw our attention back to what is positive—God himself and the hope we have in him. Just like positive space is the focal point or subject matter of a piece of art or interior room, God is our positive space, the main focal point of our lives as well. There's nothing more positive or more fulfilling than the personhood and ways of our God. Death, grief, and loss help us learn and live this, enabling us to find our hope and restoration in him. When we fill the negative space in our hearts with the positive of God, we will be able to uncover the purposes of God when life doesn't go as planned.

My dear friend Becky has walked through quite a bit of heartache. But she has chosen to lean into her grief as she continues to mourn the loss of her dad. She and I have logged many hours on Voxer sharing about those we've lost and the numerous ways God continues to comfort us. Here is a portion of what she has learned from the negative space in her own redesigned life.

The Ache of Remembrance

Becky Keife

I expect to cry on my dad's birthday. I expect the tides of grief to start rolling in around the anniversary of his death, unsettling my soul like sand slowly sinking where I stand. I expect the weight of loss to crash hard like rhythmic markers signaling another year gone by since my father's passing. It makes sense to weep when I think back to the day my sister called, confirming what I somehow knew in my gut to be true. Seven years have gone by, but it's like I'm right back in the living room of our little blue house, crumpled on the floor, rocking my baby and toddler with each heaving sob. How could he be gone?

I expect sad things to be sad. But grief doesn't stick to the rhythm of our own making—at least I haven't figured out how to make it play by my rules. If it did, the ache wouldn't sneak up on me in places like amusement parks and baseball games.

My family recently had the gift of going to Disneyland. While my sons threw their arms up in Thunder Mountain thrill and licked cinnamon sugar off their lips—oh, the glory of warm churros—a lump of grief rose in my throat. When my seven-year-old asked with sparkly eyes if the hippos on the Jungle Cruise were real, I smiled wide yet fought the tears welling behind my eyes. My dad loved Disneyland. He was a serious person in many ways, somber, often closed off. But somehow the roller coasters and stage shows, parades and clam chowder bread bowls brought out a tender lightness and generosity of spirit I seldom saw elsewhere. He would have loved going to Disneyland with my boys.

Last night my oldest son stood on the pitcher's mound in his first Little League playoff game. Nine years old, tall and lean and strong—such a different picture from the tiny toddler with blond ringlets my dad knew. With every pitch and catch and crack of the bat, my chest tightened, my breath caught shallow. Oh, how my dad loved baseball. He was always happy to show me the black-and-white yearbook photos of his high school team and spent who knows how many long evenings at Angel Stadium enjoying salty peanuts and America's favorite pastime. The thought of my dad proudly cheering on his grandson made me want to sob.

These aren't the first times that sweet and celebratory moments have stirred my heart toward grief. There was the birth of my youngest son, graduation from grad school, and a promotion at work. But the happy-turned-achy still catches me by surprise. I resist it. I don't want the joy of the present to be tainted by the loss of the past. I want to separate blessing from sorrow. Stuff down the hard so I can fully savor the good. But God doesn't compartmentalize our hearts. Loss doesn't stay in its own tidy box. It seeps into all areas of our lives. And I'm learning to recognize that the ache of remembrance for what was—or what should have been—is actually an invitation to press into the One who understands my grief. I'm learning that when I give myself permission to feel the pain instead of dismissing it, I'm able to acknowledge the gift of then and now.

Without the aching hole, I wouldn't remember to give thanks for so many wonderful memories with my dad. Without the aching hole, I wouldn't be as grateful for the blessings of my husband, children, and wonderful friends who come alongside me to champion and cheer both the daily joys and joyous milestones. And without the grief, I honestly wouldn't be as mindful of heaven. The ache of loss reminds me that this life is so very temporary and that we were created for so much more. I long for the days of eternal glory in my heavenly Father's presence—and the hope of seeing my earthly father face-to-face again.

Death was not part of God's original design. It's certainly not part of my plans either. But, in his faithfulness, God meets us in the ache. All we have to do is lean in.

Space within the Pages of Scripture

When I started to think through the principle of space and something that creates what we would consider to be negative space in our heart, I immediately thought of death. For me, the loss of certain dreams and relationships, as well as my mother's death, has left holes in my heart. I feel incredibly empty sometimes. I bet you feel the same as the result of death or the loss of anything in your life—whether a job, a dream, or a relationship.

The death and loss of someone we love is something all of us experience, making it the natural topic of countless poems and songs. Even Hollywood has produced movies like *Ghost*, *Beaches*, and *Steel Magnolias*, all of which make me bawl my face off every time I watch them. Many books have been written on death as well, by people with a bunch of letters behind their names. All of these things bring us some comfort as we grapple with the inevitability of our own death or the death of those we love. But as Becky mentioned in her story, death was not part of God's original plan for our lives. I know this because the Bible has some things to say about the death of God's children and the purpose of grief. While death is hard to understand and accept from a human perspective, here is some of what we know in regard to God's perspective on death and loss:

The death of God's children is precious to him. Death is our enemy; God is not our enemy.

I think one of the most beautiful verses in all of the Bible is Psalm 116:15, which says, "Precious in the sight of the LORD is the death of his faithful servants." We know that God weeps with us. Jesus wept over the death of his friend Lazarus (John 11:35) and is noted for being a "a man of suffering, and familiar with pain" (Isa. 53:3). How comforting it is to know that God understands and relates to our sorrow!

You may also believe or feel that death is one of the ways God punishes those who love him. While the Bible teaches that the payment for sin is death, Jesus paid this price for our sin on the cross, dying in our place for our sin. No condemnation remains then for a believer in Christ. Death is a result of a believer living in a world plagued with the effects of sin.

Death was not an original part of Adam and Eve's life in the Garden of Eden. It didn't exist until after the fall and only because of their rebellion. From that day forward, death became the enemy, robbing the lives of those made in God's image. One day death will be destroyed, however, and Jesus will reign forever and ever (1 Cor. 15:26, 54–56; Rev. 20:14). How glorious this will be!

Our grief and loss enable us to love like Jesus and to be acquainted with him in his sufferings.

It still baffles me that Jesus left heaven to dwell with people on earth. What is even more puzzling is that the human part of Jesus was made perfect "through suffering" (Heb. 2:10 ESV) and that he "learned obedience through what he suffered" (Heb. 5:8 ESV).

If Jesus became obedient and was made perfect through sufferings, then you can bet this is one of the reasons God allows us to experience grief and loss. These are part of our sanctification, making us more like Christ. I have experienced loss changing me and those around me for the better. We're more sympathetic to the pain of others as a result of it, and we become more aware of the preciousness of life and of what truly matters. And we learn to trust and love God even when our heart is breaking and when things happen that we do not understand.

> *If Jesus became obedient and was made perfect through sufferings, then you can bet this is one of the reasons God allows us to experience grief and loss.*

So for reasons like these, we can truly rejoice in the midst of our grief and loss. And when it is time for us to die, we are promised that we will be glorified completely with Christ in our death (Rom. 8:17; 1 Pet. 4:13).

God is a God who gives, comforts, and restores back to those who grieve and experience loss.

God is the ultimate Positive—full of love, goodness, justice, kindness, wisdom, patience, peace, joy, and a whole bunch of other wonderful attributes. In other words, God is positively indescribable! He promises that when we seek him with our whole heart he will be found by us (Jer. 29:13).

We already discussed how God is present in our lives and how he wishes to communicate with us in the chapter on the principle of pattern. Not only is God our great Communicator, he is also our gracious Comforter. When we cry out to God, we are asking him to fill the negative space in our heart with his comfort, strength, peace, or wisdom. I can attest to the fact that in moments of my deepest grief I have called out to God, asking for his help. In the days and months that followed my mother's passing, I experienced some of the sweetest moments of his comfort and his closeness. Perhaps you have had a similar experience. When we come to him with our loss, when we offer him the gaping hole in our heart, he will fill it with his peace, love, strength, or hope. How can he not since he is described as the God of all comfort (2 Cor. 1:3)?

When God comforts us, we're able to get up in the morning and make it through another day. And the months and years after that. This doesn't mean we're happy or that our depression suddenly vanishes, but somehow we make it. Via God's use of the principle of space, we smile again and find new purpose and strength in the wake of our losses.

God has given us pops of color to live out. Death and loss, and the space they leave within us, help make our particular color or emphasis brighter and more productive since we learn from them and become stronger from them. God not only comforts and fills us with his strength to continue onward, he also restores and gives back to those who have lost something or someone, causing them to shine brightly in a world blanketed in gray.

Though I've lost my mother, God has given me older women in the church who guide and love me in her absence. These women continue to help me to keep going in my marriage, ministry, or in motherhood whenever grief starts to overwhelm me.

I've also wept and prayed with precious friends who have lost babies. And I've smiled with joy as I watched these same friends become pregnant again and become mamas, or watched as God grew their families through adoption. Their stories and testimonies to the faithfulness of God prove that he brings new life from death and that he will bless and comfort those who mourn.

The longer I wrestle with and embrace the truths we just looked at, the more I see the beauty and purpose behind all the pain I endure and the pain those I love endure. Yes, some of my dreams have died and are still dead. My mother is still home in heaven too. But as God continues to redesign my life, he fills the empty places in my heart with himself, his promises, and the newness of unexpected blessings and people.

Why Negative Space Matters

> Even though I walk
> through the darkest valley,

I will fear no evil,
    for you are with me;
your rod and your staff,
    they comfort me. (Ps. 23:4)

The Bible has much to say about death and our God within its pages. I pray specifically for those of you who are in the midst of grieving loss of any kind, that these words will somehow bring comfort to you. I am truly sorry for your loss.

Just like negative space plays a vital role on the printed page or in the interior layout of our homes, it also plays a vital and needed role within us as well. I trust that God will help you find your way as you meander through your losses and that he will restore your joy and your strength as you come to him seeking them. I am not a grief expert, nor am I trying to dismiss the loss you are feeling.

I am in the valley with you.

But I refuse to be defined by the valley, and I am growing in my appreciation of its depths and of its beauty. The valley is where I have found my faith to be genuine and to be my guide when I cannot see. When the negative quenches the warm and fuzzy, my faith nudges me to cling tighter to my creative Creator. And so I do. He is everything to me. He is the positive space or the focal point of my life.

When others hear my mother's story they sometimes ask me if I am scared of death or dying in the manner that my mom did. No, not anymore. I watched my mother hold on to the same truths we just looked at until the very end of her life. She died well with her eyes glued on her God. Now I also know how to die well. So I no longer fear death but am embracing the days I have left instead, knowing that my figurative bags are packed in the corner too. The same is true for you, fellow traveler.

Is God the focal point of your life even though you have faced loss of some kind that you didn't design or want? What are you trying to fill the negative space in your heart with? Yes, I am asking you to consider these oh-so-uplifting questions because death and grief are the toughest things we will face in this life. I don't want you to be surprised by them or taken out of the game because of them. We can try to fill the negative space with more relationships, alcohol, shopping, Netflix, food, or more work, but things like these will never completely fulfill us like God can.

You and I are needed in this world. We cannot stop living even though things or people that we love are dying.

It's one thing to see a shiny-happy Christian bounce into a church building with a plate of cookies and bag of highlighters, posting memes and selfies from Bible study. It's a whole other thing to hear women in the pit of despair and loss say the name of Jesus with hope and love and watch them continue to trust him, proclaiming his truths with everything they've got left. Something powerful and needed happens when we comfort others with the same truth and comfort that God has poured into our hearts (2 Cor. 3–4).

Comfort is so needed in this world.

So is the gospel truth.

Give others comfort and this truth, broken one.

Give them.

You and I are needed in this world. We cannot stop living even though things or people that we love are dying.

I want us to be the kind of couture children who continue on, no matter what. Ones who while clinging to Christ in the midst of loss cover others with the same comfort we have received from him. Do not let your grief go to waste or wish it away. We cannot cover others with comfort if we have not received comfort ourselves. We cannot know the blessedness of receiving comfort either if something or someone has not been taken away from us first.

Maybe the ultimate point of death is not loss but restoration of life. Maybe the point of loss is to show us that all is actually *not* lost. While the things of this earth fade away, our God never will. The more we allow loss to change our perspective, the more we will experience God's comfort and his sufficiency, just like my friend Becky testified. And whether we find ourselves fighting back tears at a baseball game or while at Disneyland, the smile that has gone missing from our face will be found again.

twelve

Dying Well

I wish you could've met my mother, Roxie, or Foxy Roxie, as those of us who love her call her. She was diagnosed with breast cancer in her early fifties. After being in remission for five and a half years, her cancer returned. It continued to spread into some of her organs, bones, and then into her brain. The doctors believed she wouldn't make it to my wedding. But she did. They also said she probably wouldn't be around for the births of my children, but she was. What doctors said was impossible, God made possible. Cancer does not have the final say, God does. There are limitations to what science and medications can do. There are NO limitations to what our God can do.

Hours before she died, I stood beside her bed and sang "Amazing Grace" and "Jesus Loves Roxie." I knew she heard me, for her expression calmed at the sound of my voice. What a beautiful moment that I shall cherish forever. My heart was at peace as I realized that her eyes would soon behold God's glory in its fullest sense.

At around 1:15 p.m., a dear friend called, and I stepped out into the hallway to talk with her. According to my call log, I returned eleven minutes later.

Eleven minutes.

That was it.

My life changed forever. My mother had died. Her death has left a deep void within me. Death does that to all of us. Even the dying of a relationship, material possessions, career, or a dream cuts deeply and takes away our happiness, security, even our identity.

In the months that followed my mother's death I really struggled with how to move forward. Cancer had become such a part of my daily thoughts and life that I really didn't know how to live without its disgusting fingerprints all over my thoughts. The same was true with my grief. It permeated my emotions and my thoughts. I just wanted to feel happy again, like my mother asked me to do during one of our last conversations.

But the happiness was not there at the beginning. The sight of pink ribbons and the phrase *new normal* made my stomach nauseous. All the money going to research and cures did nothing to save my mother. And I didn't want a *new normal*, whatever that meant anyway.

Still today, grief sometimes overwhelms me and I miss my mother greatly. My *normal* should include my mother helping me raise my children. I'm supposed to be able to call her when

I get stuck writing a chapter of this book. She would have prayed with me and helped me with the edits, and she would have squealed at the sight of the book cover.

But I'm raising my children without her. Foxy Roxie's phone is disconnected. She utters no more prayers for me and has no idea that I'm even writing this book and that the cover turned out to be absolutely delightful.

All I have left of my mother is her memory. How I wish you could have met her, for she was a wonderful woman who loved Jesus. But one of the things I loved most about my mom was that she would always sign her name with a smiley face. In fact, she had a smiley face toaster and shirts and mugs with smiley faces on them; even her classroom had its share of the famous emoji all over it. On the day we celebrated her life I wore a bright yellow dress with a smiley face pin and a bright yellow pair of flip-flops because my mother loved yellow smiley faces so much. This beloved emoji symbolizes her legacy. She made the hearts and faces of her doctors, nurses, students, friends, and family smile. What type of legacy do you hope to leave? I pray that my legacy makes the faces and hearts of many smile as well.

While the majority of my memories of my mother are positive ones, the final memories I have of her are painful, as she suffered much from the cancer and all the chemo, dying too early from a human perspective. God still has not answered my questions about why my mother suffered the way she did, and why he called her heavenward before I was ready to say goodbye to her. But I am finally at peace with this and with his silence. If my mother were still alive, this chapter would not exist. I know this now. Out of all the chapters in this book, the previous chapter and this chapter are the most precious to me because of what I have walked through and lost in order to write what I am writing to you.

I used to be afraid of the valley of the shadow of death. Now I find purpose and peace within it. God is still good in the midst of grief. And grief, though it royally stinks, is good and necessary. Never have I cried or prayed for another person who is grieving as I do now. Never has the preciousness of time and spending it with people been more evident to me. Never has my faith been stronger. And never have I loved my God more. Because it seems the deeper the loss, the more I experience his love.

> I used to be afraid of the valley of the shadow of death. Now I find purpose and peace within it. God is still good in the midst of grief. And grief, though it royally stinks, is good and necessary.

God continues to meet with me in my grief as he promised he would. He has filled me with his comfort and loved me, though I often question his purpose for bringing breast cancer into our family's story. But since my mother's death, God has restored my joy and filled my redesigned life with new dreams and new people. This does not mean my life is perfect and full of ease, but I'm making it in this world and am trying to comfort others the best way I know how as they try to make it through their own losses.

Where grief tried to put a period in my life I now put a smiley face instead, figuratively and literally. When I write a personal note or post something to social media, you can bet there will be a smiley face or two (or several) at the end of my words.

And now you know why this is.

Recognizing Restoration after Loss

Let's look at one last person from the pages of the Old Testament who was in the thick of grief and who was honest with God about it. This particular man not only lived well, he died well too. His name was Job. He lost it *all*. His livelihood, health, family. I am guessing the losses Job experienced weren't part of his plans. No, they were part of Satan's desires for Job. Satan took them from him (Job 1:8–22; 2:3–7).

Job had some well-meaning friends who arrived on the scene and tried to discuss Job's plight with him, but they were of no help to poor Job. Like most of us in the midst of grief and loss, Job had to face and question God alone. Job was a righteous man. God favored him. And yet, Job lost everything.

> I despise my life; I would not live forever.
>   Let me alone; my days have no meaning.
> What is mankind that you make so much of them,
>   that you give them so much attention,
> that you examine them every morning
>   and test them every moment?
> Will you never look away from me,
>   or let me alone even for an instant?
> If I have sinned, what have I done to you,
>   you who see everything we do?
> Why have you made me your target?
>   Have I become a burden to you?
> Why do you not pardon my offenses
>   and forgive my sins?
> For I will soon lie down in the dust;
>   you will search for me, but I will be no more.
>   (Job 7:16–21)

No, God never answered Job's why, but what he did reveal was Job's who—which was himself.

What I find interesting is that God did not immediately respond to Job with a Kleenex, chocolate, or condolences. Which is surprising since we know that Job was a righteous man whom God loved (Job 1:1). No, God never answered Job's *why*, but what he did reveal was Job's *who*—which was himself (Job 38–41).

I can relate to Job in this respect. I love to ask questions. And chocolate or Kleenexes do not rain down from heaven onto me either whenever I ask them. Bummer, because that would be rad. What I often hear in my heart as I ask God why are the promises of Scripture that remind me of *who my God is* as my tears fall. And this is communicated not in condemnation toward me but in an effort to comfort me.

Never will I leave you nor forsake you . . . though you walk through the deep waters, I will not allow them to overtake you . . . (see Heb. 13:5; Isa. 43:2)

I am close to the brokenhearted . . . (see Ps. 34:18)

I have plans to give you hope and a future . . . (see Jer. 29:11)

In this world you will have trouble but take heart for I have overcome the world . . . (see John 16:33)

I have loved you with an everlasting love . . . (see Jer. 31:3)

I am the resurrection and the life . . . (see John 11:25)

There is a pattern here, do you see it?

I, I, I. Over and over. God is continually redirecting my focus back on to him, just like he did for Job.

The LORD blessed the latter part of Job's life more than the former part. He had fourteen thousand sheep, six thousand camels, a thousand yoke of oxen and a thousand donkeys. And he also had seven sons and three daughters. The first daughter he named Jemimah, the second Keziah and the third Keren-Happuch. Nowhere in all the land were there found women as beautiful as Job's daughters, and their father granted them an inheritance along with their brothers.

After this, Job lived a hundred and forty years; he saw his children and their children to the fourth generation. And so Job died, an old man and full of years. (Job 42:12–17)

Yes, sometimes God will provide an answer to our questions, but sometimes he just answers our questions with the truth of who he is. How did Job respond to God's revelations? He repented and continued to love and trust his God. Job could have pulled away from God as a result of his discouragement and grief, but he didn't. Job inserted his own smiley face of faith where grief intended to put a period of discouragement.

In the end, God restored Job. He filled his life back up with new blessings. I imagine that Job's face was smiling once again because of God's faithfulness. I am no longer depressed when I think of Job's story because now I see it as one of restoration, and his example and my God inspire me.

My friend Holly is also an inspiration to me. She has gone from feeling alone in her grief to feeling alive again in her faith, and has seen God restore joy within her. Be encouraged by what grief is teaching her and by the very verse that brings her hope:

I knew when my father passed I would experience horrible grief, but I was not prepared for the finality and totality of it. I found the silence of grief deafening. As people went on with their lives, I felt alone in my grief and felt that God was the only one who understood my pain. I searched the Scriptures looking for comfort and I came upon this verse in Psalm 126:6: "Those who go out weeping, carrying seed to sow, will return with songs of joy, carrying sheaves with them." Grief may be part of our journeys, but it is not our final destination. We can choose to move forward with it, to let our heavenly Father use it to sow goodness and transform our lives and those around us. We will mourn and weep, sometimes for a long while, but may we keep looking up as we journey home sowing seeds of hope and knowing this: our joy and harvest are coming.

~Holly Haynes

Ways to Experience Joy When We Weep

As Holly explained, it is possible for those who weep to experience joy again, even though this often seems and feels impossible at some points in our grief journey. Loss and death interrupt our plans, causing us to weep and wobble. But seasons of despair and shock are exactly the right times for us to turn to God, our focal point, and trust he is using grief to redesign us. The negative space that death creates within us causes us to pause and seek answers, or love that was lost, or comfort—all of which are ultimately found in the positive space or personhood of God. He is everything that we need, and God uses this principle to restore balance to the brokenhearted.

God's purpose for brokenness is to better us.

We become better or restored by filling ourselves up with him. This is why I believe that death isn't ultimately about loss, but about restoring us back into a deeper, more fulfilling relationship with God. So how can we experience joy or fill ourselves up with God when we become drained with grief? Here are some things that have helped me:

- *Owning your grief and allowing yourself to mourn openly before your God.* God wants to commune with us even when we are not at our best. Meet with him, even if your sorrow makes you want to hide under your cozy bed comforter. You cannot be filled with God's comfort or strength when you bury your feelings from the only One who can help you work through them. Jesus wept at the tomb of his friend Lazarus (John 11:35). He did not run from God, but grieved in front of his Father, God, and in front of those who were watching him. This implies that it's okay for those of us who love Jesus to grieve openly before our God and to be honest about our sadness with those around us. Don't stuff your feelings or pretend your grief isn't there. Find trusted and godly friends, support groups, or counseling professionals to help you process your emotions and plan your next steps. Do not isolate, but let others into your grief. Remember that no one will completely understand the depths of the loss you are feeling, save Jesus. So give grace to those who are trying to help and love you through your loss, and admit to Jesus and to yourself that you are hurting. There is great freedom in this.

- *Recognizing what you miss most about the person or thing that you lost.* Is it their love, companionship, or their humor that you miss the most? Or if the loss concerns your health, a certain dream, goal, or job, do you miss the sense of purpose, security, or the sense of being known that this thing would have given or did give you? Know what it is you are missing the most. Then discover if God can provide whatever it is that you miss most about that person or thing. I bet the answer will be yes! Find and meditate on verses in the Bible that promise God can do so. Ask God to fill you up with his joy and a new sense of purpose, or to fill you with his love or encouragement just like your old job or loved one did. Then wait for him to do so. This isn't a one-time ask or filling either. We are human. Certain things like a song, picture, or the holidays can trigger our grief. As I write this, my mother has been dead for six years. I am still asking God to encourage me and remind me of my worth and value, since she always did this and since certain things continue to remind me of her absence.

- *Extending comfort to others when it is time to pop.* Grief knows no time frame. It certainly doesn't behave like a bunch of outlined steps on a flowchart. All of us grieve differently. We need to give each other the grace to do so. What is helpful to realize is that God is using space in our redesigned lives to equip us to provide hope and comfort to those who are also grieving. Don't be surprised if you come in contact with someone who is experiencing the same kind of loss you are or have experienced. They may be living on adrenaline. Help them to live on assurance and point them back to God if he calls you to do so. Knowing that we've helped someone else to smile again is pretty fulfilling, isn't it? We will be blessed, because we'll realize that the tears we cry and the wisdom or comfort gleaned from them is not just for us. We experienced them providentially for the weeping or brokenhearted person that God's movement places in front of us. God may design for us to pop in this sacred way so that someone else can make it through another hour when they'd rather be hiding under their cozy bed comforter. These are holy moments. Our arms are not here to hold Prada. They are here to hold hurting people.

Being honest, asking God to fill you with what you lack, and comforting others with the comfort you've received from God yourself are ways that you open yourself up to being filled and blessed when grief is draining you.

Your Loss Matters to God

God will do something similar in our lives as he did for Job, although it may not mean he will give us all our fortunes back or double all that we have (see Job 42:10). Our blessings may include these things, but they may look different and will be according to God's one-of-a-kind, couture designs for our lives.

And just look at how many lives Job's story continues to touch. He had no idea God would use his suffering in the way he has. The same is true for us. We have no idea how God will use our suffering to touch the lives of those around us. Our God wastes nothing. He places us within community and gives us tools like social media so we can share and testify to the goodness and comfort of God with those around us in person or online like never before. So what will we do with the awesome responsibility of sharing God and with the honor of comforting others? I pray we steward it well. When we stay the course, our faces will smile again, and as my friend Holly said, our God *will* harvest from our seasons of brokenness.

This is why your grief matters. What or who you have lost matters. I know this is not what you want or had planned on happening. And I also know the pain of watching others go on as if they have lost nothing, while you have lost everything. Maybe the person or the thing you have lost no longer matters to the world, but your losses still matter to God because he allows them to be part of his design for your life. Seasons of grief are among the finest we will live. They are not the most fun, but they are some of the finest.

Be comforted and encouraged. Do not despair or compare—none of our losses will look the same. Our grief is individual because we are couture. No one can completely understand what you are going through, because he or she wasn't designed to understand! God is the only One who understands you because he is the positive space that your heart encircles. He is the only One who can ultimately comfort you and fill the negative or empty spaces within your heart. Allow your pain to point you back to the positive God who loves you.

> Maybe the person or the thing you have lost no longer matters to the world, but your losses still matter to God because he allows them to be part of his design for your life.

No matter the diagnosis. No matter how many relationships or dreams die.

Fix your eyes on the Focal Point. Fill yourself up with him.

One day you will meet Jesus face-to-face.

Die well.

Muse Minutes

1. To help cement principle #6 into that beautiful mind and heart of yours, rewrite in your own words what *space* is here.

   Rewrite in your own words how God uses this principle in our lives.

2. Has God comforted you in the midst of your past or recent loss? Have you felt his comfort or strength or peace as you grieve? Write down two or three ways you can share this same comfort with those around you.

3. What does dying well look like or mean to you? What type of legacy do you hope to leave?

DESIGN TIP
for Your Home: Lines

Horizontal lines help spaces to feel stable, secure, and restful. If you want your home to feel comfy, consider utilizing horizontal lines or furnishings such as beds, tables, or couches throughout. Also note that the horizontal lines of molding or chair rails placed on walls at the same height help adjacent spaces to feel connected to each other and help lead the eye along to a focal point in the room.[1]

Vertical lines, however, are not as relaxing. They make our eyes travel upward and can make a room feel taller or more formal. Vertical lines also help lift the spirit, which is why most churches and the great cathedrals of old used vertical lines in their architecture. So if you are in the home-building or renovating stage and you want to convey strength or grandness in rooms like your formal living room or entryway, think about how to accent the vertical lines in these spaces through the use of taller windows or columns.[2]

And don't forget about diagonal or curved lines too. Curved lines evoke a sense of femininity and diagonal lines nurture a sense of excitement.[3] So consider the littlest of lines whenever you are designing or redesigning your home. They are more powerful than you think!

A Redesigned Life

Here we are at the end of our trek between the covers of this book. My heart is scattered all over the pages you just read. How I wish I could sit across from you and hear slices of your story. We would probably chuckle a lot or need some tissues as we talk. I bet parts of your story sound eerily similar to parts of my story. This is by design. *God's* design, that is. And he sure is redesigning us, isn't he?

I pray that *A Redesigned Life* has made you chuckle in some places and reflect in others. I hope it has helped you notice something spectacular about the God who loves you and about your own couture calling. Your life has such a unique beauty of its own. You are greatly needed in this world.

Yes, there will be some who will yawn at us, measuring our worth or our wisdom by their own standards. But God sees, values, and uses what the world dismisses, rejects, and discards. He will see each of us through plans we did not design.

God sees, values, and uses what the world dismisses, rejects, and discards.

This life is full of shocks and surprises, but hang on. Be encouraged. The Bible promises that there will be no more death or grief for those who are in heaven for all of eternity. There will be no more lost pink tutus or broken dreams either. No more fails will happen in heaven as a result of bizarre Pinterest recipes or motherhood in general. Our efforts to be an all-red room will cease. And our hearts and minds will be completely healed, allowing us to finally grasp the significance of God's movement in our lives in its fullest sense (1 Cor. 13:12). Trust God in the midst of what doesn't make sense now. Your eternal aha moment is coming.

I don't want you to give up or miss seeing the loving hand of God move in your life. Let go of unrealistic expectations. Laugh. Love like a Jonathan would. Be someone's Hannah. Forgive and forgive some more. Enjoy the weirdness and divine coincidence. Love much because you have been forgiven much. Grieve. Put a smiley face where loss intends to put a period. Live on assurance and die well.

As you come to the end of this book, I hope your faith and trust in God are renewed and strengthened. God is still beyond what we can even think or imagine. He will move in ways that are beyond what I have presented to you here.

Yes, some of life's surprises and disappointments will remain mysterious and unexplainable. But most often, if we take the time, we will be able to notice God's involvement and rest in it, allowing us to find contentment in the midst of living a life we did not expect or design.

So couture child of the King, remember the design principles we discussed during our time together. They will help turn your focus back to God. And they will give you a fresh, creative way to uncover his purposes and to remember the preciousness and prevalence of God's presence in your life. Remember:

- **Movement** happens whenever an edge of rejection or a curve of surprise catches your attention. God is using these to direct the eyes of your heart back to him, the intended focal point of your life.

- **Emphasis** appears when you use your God-given, unique pop of color to love and serve those around you. God uses the process of sanctification to grow, stretch, and mature us, and to reveal the specifics of our emphasis.

- **Pattern** is displayed when God uses repetition in your life to catch your attention, teach you, or help you remember who he is and what he desires for your life.

- **Contrast** occurs when God brings people and circumstances into your life that are the opposite of you, or opposite of what you'd hoped for, in order to help you see him and yourself more clearly.

- **Balance** is evident when everything in your heart and relationships looks and feels right. If there is something negative going on in any of these areas, God will allow you to feel wobbly inside so you can fix whatever is off and restore balance or harmony in your relationship with him or with those around you.

- **Space** is present whenever loss and grief leave a hole in your heart. God uses space to give you permission to pause and reevaluate and ultimately draw your attention back to what is positive—God himself and the hope you have in him.

Remember these six design principles going forward. They are all around us. Look for them, consider them some more, and smile—because this girl from Kansas is going to do the same.

From obscure to couture.

My name is Tracy Steel.

I am living a life I did not design, but one that God is redesigning for me.

And I am enjoying it and overwhelmed by it in the best possible way. ☺

Come and Sit
on the Couch

As an interior designer, I worked hard to meet the needs of my clients and to create spaces of beauty and function for them. After the paint had dried and the furnishings were put into place, I always did a final walk-through of a new space to ensure everything was properly placed and in working order. Scratches in the wood? I looked for them. A loose string on the fabric? I cut it. A smudge on the glass? I cleaned it. If all was as it should be, then my designer's heart was at peace. I knew that what I was turning over to my clients was beautiful and efficient, ready to serve them and be enjoyed by them. I went the extra mile for my clients because I cared and because I wanted them to be pleased with what they had purchased.

While I am pleased with what I have designed for you in this book, my heart is not yet at peace. I long for every single one of you to have an eternal peace and to enjoy a relationship with your creative Creator. I care about the scratches, the loose strings, and the smudges in your lives. Here is one last invitation from me to you. I pray you'll come and finally sit down on the white couch.

———

I realize some of you believe the things of faith and of God himself to be purely speculative or fictitious. I also realize that some of you are walking through a deep loss of some kind, so you are angry at God or refuse to believe he could even exist. How could a good God allow the horrors that have been done to you or to someone you love or the evils that exist in the world around you? Or maybe there is another reason why you continue to run from God or deny his existence.

Precious one, you are welcome here. I do not pretend to understand your pain or your doubt. I only know that I have doubted God. I have stood with him in the various hallway seasons of my life lost and confused. I have thought the Bible to be a bunch of buffoonery. I have lost much. There were certain seasons of my life when all I could see were scratches and a ton of smudges. There was no peace in my heart. Evil was done to those I love. So I kept running from God. But after a while, I started feeling uneasy for doing so. I kept trying to push him away, but there were reminders of God everywhere. And it scared me. I am no Mother Theresa. How could God possibly love me? I really believed that God couldn't and wouldn't love me because of some of the things I had done and continued to do.

But over time I felt increasingly drawn to him. I can't describe it. I saw other people who weren't like Mother Theresa being loved by him and loving him back. I wanted the security and peace they had, because I had tried everything else that this world promises would make me whole and make me somebody.

And it wasn't working. Heck, the world still yawns at me, but this no longer bugs me. I am loved deeply by God, and I am whole in the sense that he *does* provide all that I need. A relationship with Jesus Christ has made all the difference. Jesus *is* the way, the truth, and the life (John 14:6).

I long for you to be whole in Christ and for you to experience his love. And the good news is that Jesus will never turn away anyone who comes to him asking to be forgiven, like the unnamed women we looked at in this book. God *will* pick you back up and begin to wipe away the smudges, heal the scratches, and cut you free from all the loose strings that have kept you tripped up and bound up for years. He will do so because he cares and because God is proud of what he purchased through the blood of his son, Jesus, which is *you* (1 Cor. 6:19–20). Do you believe this? While you may feel scared to love this God that you just read about, would you give a relationship with him a chance?

God sees you. He loves you. Jesus came to this earth, suffered, was crucified, died, buried, and then rose again on the third day (1 Cor. 15:3–5). His death and resurrection satisfied the wrath of God against *all* our sins—past, present, and future. Whoever asks for forgiveness of their sins and asks Jesus to be their Lord and Savior *will be saved* (John 3:16; Rom. 10:9). Receive the Lord and you will be saved. By faith. For good. Forever.

Salvation is a gift found only in him and through him; it is never a result of trying harder or doing more. It is by faith alone (Eph. 2:8–10). And I believe that today is a perfect day for you to stop running and to confess and believe.

There is still time for you to join me on the figurative white couch, come before the throne of God's grace, and worship him. For all are welcome to come and receive the sufficient and sustaining grace and forgiveness of God. And if you do decide to give God a chance and receive Jesus as your Savior, I encourage you to reach out to a Christian friend or family member or to find a place that teaches the Bible so that you can meet other brothers and sisters who love Jesus and who can help you grow in your faith.

And now as I finish my final walk-through of *A Redesigned Life,* my designer's heart is finally at peace. I have written this to you because I care. Know that I am praying for you, and some of you by name.

Come and take a seat on the white couch.

Welcome home to your redesigned life.

God is waiting with his arms opened wide.

Acknowledgments

To my readers and to Kaitlyn and my launch team ladies: I count it the highest honor to pray for you, to mourn with you, and to celebrate the successes that have also been yours. I thank God for you, your prayers, for every like, post share, and comment, and for your efforts in helping me launch this book. I cannot thank you enough. You are loved and appreciated more than you know.

To Patti Brinks, Eileen Hanson, Brian Brunsting, Gisèle Mix, Julie Davis, and the team at Revell: It's been an honor to work with you. Thank you for not being ashamed of the gospel and for using your God-given talents to ensure that this message reaches the hearts of women. My deepest thanks for everything.

To my acquisitions editor, Kelsey Bowen: How can I ever thank you enough for not yawning at me? You handled the unfolding and polishing of my heart upon these pages with such grace and wisdom. You are brilliant and I love how we *always* end up laughing about something.

To my agent, Jessica Kirkland: Thank you for your belief in this message, for your wisdom and input throughout the publishing process, and for your prayers. From shooting basketballs to pitching book proposals, you are dancing splendidly in the parts God has chosen just for you. I thank God for you, friend, and am glad I handed you a bottle of lavender lotion at *Declare.*

To Niki: We did it! What a pleasure it's been to navigate life and publishing with you. Thank you for being a loyal prayer warrior and cheerleader. I am so proud of you and of the beautiful message you just released into the world. Here's to more bows and cups of tea. I adore you.

To Shannon C., Erika, Jenet, Shannon B., Sarah, Tricia, Becky, Carey, Bobbie, Shontell, Teri Lynne, Katie, Lauren, Elizabeth, Erin, Jen, Connie, Jodi, Maria, and my fellow Build A Sister Up/Hope*Writer sisters: Thank you for being my Hannahs. Your prayers, encouragement, and counsel keep me going. I thank God for how he is redesigning each of you into couture, incredible women who shine so faithfully and beautifully for him. Keep popping, friends.

To Cat: You were the first one to encourage me to be a writer. But our lives crossed for more reasons than this, and I am grateful for *all* of them, LP. Thank you for also taking me to Buc-ee's and for educating me on the ways and wishes of introverts everywhere. Call you in five minutes . . .

To Dad, Jamers, and Grandma Betty: Thank you for your continued support. Dad—thanks for always believing in me and for always being here for me. I love you all a bushel and a peck.

To Jackson and Katie: Mommy is forever grateful to God for including the two of you in his designs for my life! May our God always be the focal point of your lives and may you thrill in the pops of color that he has designed just for you. I love you both way more than "this much."

To Chad: Thank you for believing in me more than I believe in myself and for making me feel loved and cherished. You've sacrificed much so I can pursue my dreams. Thank you for serving our country and for leading our family with integrity and wisdom. I love you, hawtie. Always.

To God, my Father, Jesus, my Savior, and to the Holy Spirit, my Counselor and Comforter: Every word in this book is for you and because of you. I feel so inadequate to even try to share about who you are and how you move in our lives. Yet, your grace has saved me and your love propels me to try. You are the strength of my heart and my portion forever. Thank you for redesigning my life. You continue to do more than I could ever imagine or think possible with this girl from Kansas. To you be the glory, honor, and praise for taking men and women who are discarded and unknown and redesigning them into loved and celebrated masterpieces. *Acts 20:24*

Notes

Chapter 1 Making God Your Focal Point

1. Teresa Bernard, "Principles of Good Design: Movement," Teresa Bernard Oil Paintings, November 6, 2012, http://teresabernardart.com/principles-of-good-design-movement/.
2. Millard J. Erickson, *Christian Theology*, 3rd ed. (Grand Rapids: Baker Academic, 2013), 358–59.
3. Erickson, *Christian Theology*, 359.

Chapter 2 Staying Steadfast When Dreams Die

1. Ross Kraemer, "Jewish Women in Graeco-Roman Palestine: An Inquiry into Image and Status," *Journal of the American Oriental Society* 118, no. 4, quoted in S. R. Papazov, "The Place of Women in the Graeco-Roman World," *Enrichment Journal*, accessed February 16, 2017, http://enrichmentjournal.ag.org/201004/201004_000_christian_women.cfm.
2. Elisabeth M. Tetlow, "The Status of Women in Greek, Roman and Jewish Society," *Women and Ministry in the New Testament* (Mahwah, NJ: Paulist Press, 1980), Wijngaards Institute for Catholic Research, accessed August 12, 2017, http://www.womenpriests.org/articles-books/the-status-of-women-in-greek-roman-and-jewish-society-by-elisabeth-m-tetlow-from-women-and-ministry-in-the-new-testament/

Chapter 3 Living Out Your Pop of Color for God

1. Donna Tersiisky, "The ABCs of Visual Design: Emphasis," accessed June 23, 2018, http://www.tersiiska.com/design/principles/.
2. Wayne Grudem, *Systematic Theology: An Introduction to Biblical Doctrine* (Leicester & Grand Rapids: InterVarsity Press & Zondervan, 1999), 746.

Chapter 4 Knowing When to Say Yes or No

1. Ellen Cheever, *Design Principles* (Hackettstown, NJ: National Kitchen & Bath Association, 2006), 74–75.
2. Rosemary Kilmer and W. Otie Kilmer, *Designing Interiors*, 2nd ed. (Hoboken, NJ: Wiley, 2014), 165.

Chapter 5 Sticking to the Instructions God Gives You

1. Rafiq Elmansy, "Design Principles: Repetition, Pattern, and Rhythm," Designorate, June 30, 2016, http://www.designorate.com/design-principles -repetition-pattern-and-rhythm/.
2. Erickson, *Christian Theology*, 122.
3. Additional passages pertaining to the pattern of forever that you may wish to study or memorize include Ps. 103:17; 145:13; Isa. 26:4; 40:28; and Rev. 11:15.
4. Additional passages pertaining to the pattern of forgiveness that you may wish to study or memorize include Isa. 1:18; Matt. 6:14–15; and Col. 3:13.
5. Additional passages pertaining to the pattern of fun that you may wish to study or memorize include Zeph. 3:17; Hab. 3:18; and Heb. 12:2.

Chapter 6 Replacing Negative Patterns in Your Life

1. I realize this is not the correct spelling of the word *hot*. But if you follow me on social media, you know I use it to describe Chad because he is so handsome that he deserves his own special spelling of "hawt." So no, this is not a typo that my amazing editor missed. Be comforted.
2. Cheever, *Design Principles*, 50.

Chapter 7 Seeing God More Clearly

1. Teresa Bernard, "Principles of Good Design: Contrast," Teresa Bernard Oil Paintings, February 10, 2013, http://teresabernardart.com/principles-of -good-design-contrast/.
2. Grudem, *Systematic Theology*, 198.
3. Grudem, *Systematic Theology*, 205–6.

Chapter 9 Experiencing Perfect Stability with God

1. Christopher Klein, "The Twin Towers High-Wire Walk, 40 Years Ago," History.com, August 7, 2014, https://www.history.com/news/the-twin -towers-high-wire-walk-40-years-ago.
2. Cheever, *Design Principles*, 76.
3. To help you grow in your understanding of the spiritual disciplines, Anna LeBaron, the contributor for this chapter, suggests reading *The Spirit*

of the Disciplines: Understanding How God Changes Lives by Dallas Willard and *Celebration of Discipline: The Path to Spiritual Growth* by Richard J. Foster. I would also suggest *Spiritual Disciplines for the Christian Life* by Donald S. Whitney.

Chaper 11 Filling Yourself with God as You Grieve

1. Teresa Bernard, "Principles of Good Design: Space," Teresa Bernard Oil Paintings, October 15, 2012, http://teresabernardart.com/principles-of-good-design-space/.

Chapter 12 Dying Well

1. Marie Grainger, "Learning the Basics—Interior Design," accessed February 23, 2019, http://aceinteriordesign.weebly.com/line.html.
2. Grainger, "Learning the Basics."
3. Grainger, "Learning the Basics."

Contributor Gallery

Special thanks to the following lovelies for sharing a slice of their story with us:

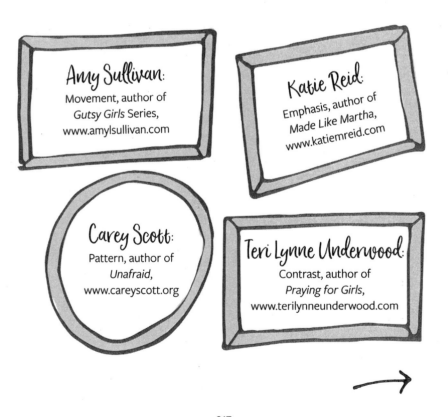

Amy Sullivan:
Movement, author of
Gutsy Girls Series,
www.amylsullivan.com

Katie Reid:
Emphasis, author of
Made Like Martha,
www.katiemreid.com

Carey Scott:
Pattern, author of
Unafraid,
www.careyscott.org

Teri Lynne Underwood:
Contrast, author of
Praying for Girls,
www.terilynneunderwood.com

→

Anna LeBaron:
Balance, author of
The Polygamist's Daughter,
www.annalebaron.com

Becky Keife:
Space, author of
*No Better Mom
for the Job,*
www.beckykeife.com

I would
also like to extend my
warmest regards to Catherine,
Erin, Gretchen, Shontell, Bobbie, Holly,
Jolene, and Varina. Your wisdom and faith
in the God who is redesigning you is an inspiration to me. Thank you for sharing pieces of
your heart with us throughout the promo
material and the pages of this book.

Abbreviations

Old Testament

Gen.	Genesis	Eccles.	Ecclesiastes
Exod.	Exodus	Song	Song of Songs
Lev.	Leviticus	Isa.	Isaiah
Num.	Numbers	Jer.	Jeremiah
Deut.	Deuteronomy	Lam.	Lamentations
Josh.	Joshua	Ezek.	Ezekiel
Judg.	Judges	Dan.	Daniel
Ruth	Ruth	Hosea	Hosea
1 Sam.	1 Samuel	Joel	Joel
2 Sam.	2 Samuel	Amos	Amos
1 Kings	1 Kings	Obad.	Obadiah
2 Kings	2 Kings	Jon.	Jonah
1 Chron.	1 Chronicles	Mic.	Micah
2 Chron.	2 Chronicles	Nah.	Nahum
Ezra	Ezra	Hab.	Habakkuk
Neh.	Nehemiah	Zeph.	Zephaniah
Esther	Esther	Hag.	Haggai
Job	Job	Zech.	Zechariah
Ps(s).	Psalm(s)	Mal.	Malachi
Prov.	Proverbs		

New Testament

Matt.	Matthew	1 Tim.	1 Timothy
Mark	Mark	2 Tim.	2 Timothy
Luke	Luke	Titus	Titus
John	John	Philem.	Philemon
Acts	Acts	Heb.	Hebrews
Rom.	Romans	James	James
1 Cor.	1 Corinthians	1 Pet.	1 Peter
2 Cor.	2 Corinthians	2 Pet.	2 Peter
Gal.	Galatians	1 John	1 John
Eph.	Ephesians	2 John	2 John
Phil.	Philippians	3 John	3 John
Col.	Colossians	Jude	Jude
1 Thess.	1 Thessalonians	Rev.	Revelation
2 Thess.	2 Thessalonians		

Tracy Steel graduated from Kansas State University with a BS in interior design in 1998. During her tenure as a project designer, Tracy created and coordinated the design and space planning of commercial spaces for clients such as Bank One, Wells Fargo, DHS, and Lockheed Martin. Since 2001 Tracy has been involved in youth and women's ministry and served as the Director of Female Students at Scottsdale Bible Church from 2005–7. In May 2019, Tracy graduated from Phoenix Seminary with a master's degree in biblical and theological studies. But Tracy is most proud of her military man and of the two spirited kiddos who call her Mama. To connect with Tracy or to inquire about her availability as a speaker for your next event, visit her online home at www.tracymsteel.com.

CONNECT WITH

Tracy

TracyMSteel.com